Who Says You Can't Teach an Old Dog New Tricks?

A COMPREHENSIVE MANUAL FOR ALL THINGS VOCATIONAL EDUCATION

The principles and andragogical philosophies of modern vocational education

DAVID W. MAYNE

First published by Busybird Publishing 2024

Copyright © 2024 David Mayne

ISBN:
Print: 978-1-923216-22-8
Ebook: 978-1-923216-23-5

This work is copyright. Apart from any use permitted under the *Copyright Act 1968*, no part of this publication may be reproduced, stored in a retrieval system or transmitted in any form or by any means, electronic, mechanical, photocopying, recording or otherwise, without the prior written permission of David Mayne.

The information in this book is based on the author's experiences and opinions. The author and publisher disclaim responsibility for any adverse consequences, which may result from use of the information contained herein. Permission to use any external content has been sought by the author. Any breaches will be rectified in further editions of the book.

Cover Image: Jeremy Bishop

Cover design: Busybird Publishing

Layout and typesetting: Busybird Publishing

Illustrations: Meg Hanlon

Busybird Publishing
2/118 Para Road
Montmorency, Victoria
Australia 3094
www.busybird.com.au

Contents

I – Preface i

II – Introduction v

III – Foreword ix

Chapter 1: Who are Your Participants? 1

Chapter 2: Andragogy and Vocational Education 17

Chapter 3: Who Should be a Vocational or Adult Educator? 21

Chapter 4: Verbal and Nonverbal Communication 29

Chapter 5: Nonverbal Communication and Body Language 39

Chapter 6: Language Structure and Form 47

Chapter 7: Safety 50

Chapter 8: Workplace Education 55

Chapter 9: Presentation and Presentation 59

Chapter 10: Suitable Suits 67

Chapter 11: Room Set-up and Configurations 71

Chapter 12: Lighting and Acoustics (The Sweet Spot) 75

Chapter 13: Public Speaking Terrors and Voice Projection 81

Chapter 14: Session Preparation 90

Chapter 15: Emotional Intelligence 93

Chapter 16: Emotional Detachment 99

Chapter 17: Dealing with Difficult Participants or Groups 103

Chapter 18: Basic Principles of Conflict Resolution and Restoration ... 128

Chapter 19: A Captive Audience 133

Chapter 20: Verbal Punctuation	141
Chapter 21: Cognitive Thought vs Intellectual Thought	146
Chapter 22: Profiling in the Educational Environment	149
Chapter 23: Audio-Visual Technology	155
Chapter 24: Video Conferencing Platforms	161
Chapter 25: On Your First Day	171
Chapter 26: Fatal Attraction	176
Chapter 27: Compliance through Policy, Procedure and Legislation	181
Chapter 28: Keeping records	189
IV: Postface	192
Acknowledgements	194
Glossary of Words, Terms and Phrases	195
Author's Quotes Throughout the Book	203
References	206

I – Preface

This book took almost forty years from inception to publication. Not because of procrastination but because the accumulation of knowledge and skills is a lifelong process, culminating in the desire to pass on that knowledge and those skills to others.

As a vocational educator who started with very little experience and even less guidance, a lot was hit and miss for me. I learned through my mistakes in my early days, but there were times when I thought I should give up and seek out another vocation. However, as I stumbled through those early years, I became more and more aware that what I was doing was in fact helping others. By virtue of this, I was helping myself not only as an educator, but also in personal growth. This led to greater confidence and proficiency in what I was doing and, most importantly, a knowledge and confidence as to why I was doing it.

I have been a public speaker from my early years and even worked in radio for several years as an 'on air' and 'off air' staff member. I also dabbled in informal training of new radio industry staff. The difference was that I was expounding my personal knowledge, skills and experience in an informal environment that required no specific learning outcomes or formal assessments.

All this early experience and informal training was vitally important in my future academic pursuits and the vocational education direction I have followed to present day. I really appreciate my early years as a volunteer in presenting knowledge and skills to others and am sincerely grateful for the many mistakes I made, as it formulated a very useful checks and balances strategy that I continue to use today. The knowledge I have gained through mistakes and advice from others who are more experienced gave me opportunity to learn and instil teaching methodologies and strategies into my own presentations.

In the beginning, I made mistakes for many reasons: I wasn't familiar with the subject matter; I didn't understand the participants' motives for undertaking their training; I had no idea what was expected of me and what I should expect from the participants. And on top of all this I felt my hands were often tied by painful compliance regulations of training providers and government bodies that oversee all accredited learning.

Looking back, I realise how crucial these formative years have been for me. I've learned so much from my mistakes and the advice from mentors with their own experience. I've had far-reaching interactions with a vast range of participants – from long-term unemployed, to highly successful business executives, to incarcerated inmates. To all these wonderful and at times inspiring people, I owe a huge debt of gratitude for being my primary teachers in vocational education.

As challenging as my early years in education were, they've given me the priceless opportunity to learn and impart teaching methodologies and strategies that are, quite simply, indispensable.

I started my vocational education career in scientific research, but after nearly twenty years I realised that I wanted to branch out into the humanities. As such I began graduate and postgraduate qualifications in organisational communications and public relations with a focus on behavioural science. This led to Leadership and Management and corporate psychology. It doesn't matter what your start in life is: if you have passion, understanding, skills, knowledge of a field of study and you would like to share these things with others, then vocational education may be for you.

Let me leave you with no delusions: you will make mistakes and you will feel like throwing it all away at times. But let me caution you in not making quick decisions based on emotions and lack of confidence.

You will find your place in vocational education, and you will reap many valuable rewards in your time as an adult educator.

You will gain more out of teaching others than you can possibly imagine and in so doing be fully aware that you are at times making significant and potentially life-altering positive changes to individuals. What you do counts and will make a difference.

Star Thrower

Once upon a time, there was an old man who used to go to the ocean to do his writing. He had a habit of walking on the beach every morning before he began his work. Early one morning, he was walking along the shore after a big storm had passed and found the vast beach littered with starfish as far as the eye could see, stretching in both directions.

Off in the distance, the old man noticed a small boy approaching. As the boy walked, he paused every so often and as he grew closer, the man could see that he was occasionally bending down to pick up an object and throw it into the sea. The boy came closer still and the man called out, 'Good morning! May I ask what it is that you are doing?'

The young boy paused, looked up, and replied, 'Throwing starfish into the ocean. The tide has washed them up onto the beach and they can't return to the sea by themselves,' the youth replied. 'When the sun gets high, they will die, unless I throw them back into the water.'

The old man replied, 'But there must be tens of thousands of starfish on this beach. I'm afraid you won't really be able to make much of a difference.'

The boy bent down, picked up yet another starfish and threw it as far as he could into the ocean. Then he turned, smiled and said, 'It made a difference to that one!'

– **Adapted from** *The Star Thrower* **(1969) by Loren Eiseley (1907 – 1977)**

'If a man picks an apple, he is fed. Give him an education and he can pick the apple without the worm.'

– **David W. Mayne**

II – Introduction

The sharing of knowledge and skills is not new. It is a process that has followed humanity through the ages. It is an evolving and, at times, non-objective process.

Mankind has always lived in groups. Sometimes they are extended families, tribes, teams, nations and even continents. In a fundamental, basic and even 'raw' sense, skills and knowledge are crucial for the survival of these groups and the individuals within them. Procreation, food, protection, shelter, environmental understanding and self-awareness: these are the primary needs for all human existence. These skills must be passed on to others for comfort and survival. Stories by campfires and drawings on cave walls served as primary education tools to enlighten others of important knowledge and skills needed for survival. One could even say this was the earliest form of vocational education!

This book aims to cover the many theoretical and practical components of vocational (adult workplace) education. In doing so, I aim to provide the vocational educator with knowledge, skills and practical applications to help them in this most rewarding of instructional vocations. These are areas that will benefit not only the new educator but also those who have been in the industry for many years and may need a refresher or even renewed inspiration.

This book not only focuses on the individual who is new to adult education but to all who impart knowledge and skills to others. This includes university professors, secondary college lecturers, and workshop and seminar facilitators. In summary: anyone sharing knowledge and skills with other adults.

The key element is to always learn from your mistakes. Never be afraid to fail and realise that the gaining of knowledge does not always equate to wisdom. It needs to be an open and ongoing journey until you breathe your last.

'Learn so that you may teach.'

– David W. Mayne

This book is a glimpse into the ever-changing world of adult education. It does not suggest empowering with absolute wisdom once the last page has been read. However, it does hope to equip the reader with possible solutions and strategies to problems and concerns that all vocational educators face at some time.

Please be assured that this author has learnt from mistakes and is continually learning from errors made. The world and its many paradigms are continually changing and evolving; therefore, what was considered the 'norm' in adult education even ten years ago is no longer considered the 'norm' today. In some cases, older practices are even seen as abhorrent and adverse to certain modern legislations and policies. As such, be prepared to change as you align with this ever-changing area of vocation.

There are certain key areas in any vocation that are skills, knowledge and understandings specific to that vocation. Fundamental skills that are the cornerstones for proficiently undertaking jobs to the satisfaction of customers, clients, bosses and, importantly, yourself. Adult and vocational education are no different.

This book covers many areas that are seen as fundamental sets of skills, knowledge and strategies to help the reader on the way to becoming the best adult educator they can be. These include: overcoming fear of public speaking, how to present yourself in various leaning environments, how to deal with difficult clients, use of language in structure and form,

Verbal and Nonverbal punctuation, reading body language, special needs education, tools to use in presentations, what to do and don't do in any learning environment, compliance and following policy and legislation and, of course, your first day nerves. All this will be covered, as well as other personal growth tools such as emotional intelligence and emotional detachment.

- The first time you read this book is important.
- The second time you read it is vital.
- The third time you read it is for reference material and refamiliarisation.
- Have a notepad or iPad beside you. Jot down points of interest or for further review.
- Relax and review and above all, remember that it's okay to make mistakes. It's how you respond to those mistakes that make you a great adult educator.

III – Foreword

David Mayne is a colossus in the world of vocational education. It is one thing to have knowledge and experience in education; it is an entirely different thing to have the skills to *impart* these attributes. David has both of these qualities in spades.

I have followed David's career in adult education for over a decade now, and like so many, I've come to thoroughly admire his command of his craft. I have watched him guide, tutor and mentor multitudes of students over the years, and I've been in awe to see so many of their lives transformed.

When David approaches an audience, he has a presence about him that commands their full attention. Watching him and listening to him address a gathering, you would assume that this man is a *natural* – he's been born with these exceptional gifts of communication. But it's fascinating to learn that these precious skills are not innate – they are *learned* – through education and life experience. David has been generous enough to share these skills and his own life lessons that have led him to become the highly sought-out public speaker, the educator, the outstanding raconteur that he is.

I spend much of my life as an educator of undergraduate and postgraduate medical students and doctors, and for years I felt there was nothing I needed to do to improve in my teaching and mentoring techniques. But to my wonderful surprise, I found David's book to be an invaluable asset to me to refine and improve my educational style. As a result, my own students have benefited enormously.

I highly recommend this book to vocational educators old and new, and to students and participants in adult education who wish to get the very best out of their educational experience.

– **Associate Professor Raymond Hodgson**

Chapter 1

Who are Your Participants?

'It was the best of times. It was the worst of times.'

– *A Tale of Two Cities* (1859), Charles Dickens

There are many factors that determine who does vocational education and why. These can be a mandatory workplace requirement, workplace or institution behaviour correction (disciplinary action), the individual's desire for personal growth, another's advice through external observation, a 'stepping stone' to progress professionally or academically, or an interest in a specific subject. In most cases the desire for professional promotion with the prospect of an increased salary is a primary motivating force.

To know who your participants are is to understand that everyone has a different story. You don't know their background or history or what has brought them to this point in their lives before you in a learning environment now.

Never prejudge a participant. You are there for the sole purpose of providing knowledge, skills and understanding. You don't know the path they have trod that has shaped who they are now. Never expect to step into their shoes to gain understanding but at least admire their footwear. If you are fortunate enough to continue as an adult educator, then throughout your career you will recognise the personalities and formative experiences of the individuals set out in following profiles.

In these profiles, you will recognise experiences and traits that may be found in your own participants or audiences. Don't take these for granted. They are a learning tool that is invaluable as you travel this road as an adult/vocational educator.

Throughout this book, you will be able to cross reference elements of the individual profiles below with identification, awareness and potential ways to address possible issues or situations.

Cheryl

42-year-old Cheryl stopped at the doorway to the training room and froze. She was about to start a journey that she never imagined she would make.

Earlier that morning Cheryl faced her pokey bathroom mirror. The new, strange silence in her small flat made her pause and consider the life change she'd recently chosen.

No kids now – they've all started on their own bumpy journeys. No significant man in her life – a monumental change from her constant stream of lovers. Monthly lovers, sometimes weekly. Lovers who were surely keepers. Keepers, that these days, seemed to spoil even more quickly.

Cheryl studied her cheerless reflection and the deepening lines of her face. 'So why would any decent man want me in his life?' she whispered to the surly pout that stared back, 'I'm a failure. I hate this life.'

An hour later, and now a few blocks from the training room, Cheryl parked her battered '98 Commodore. Her car space was handy: close enough to walk, but far enough to avoid the city parking meters – or worse, a parking fine – something there was no way she could afford.

She slowly edged the car into the space, careful not to scratch the Duco of the shiny BMW parked in front. She sat there, car idling, and contemplated the huge step she was about to take. The Commodore coughed and spluttered as if in its final gasps of life. She switched off the struggling engine and sat for a few more minutes to draw in some deep breaths. She grabbed her handbag, slammed the car door, and willed herself down the street in the direction of the Registered Training Centre.

The receptionist greeted Cheryl with a warm smile.

'She smirked at me,' Cheryl thought to herself. 'That was definitely a smirk. She thinks I don't belong here, I'm sure of it. Coming here was a mistake.'

Slowly, reluctantly she climbed the stairs to the training room.

At the doorway now, her legs anchored to the floor, her heart racing as she scanned the training room. Half a dozen people inside, all sitting at tables configured in a horseshoe shape. Most were tapping on mobile phones or fossicking through papers, no one talking.

'Most of these people look about my age,' Cheryl thought. 'But they all look so serious and smart. I wish I was more like them.'

Slowly, Cheryl inched her way into the room and chose a seat next to a middle-aged woman. The woman, head down, texting, acknowledged Cheryl with a sideways glance and a brisk nod.

As Cheryl sat down, a new fear possessed her. 'It's been years since I studied,' she thought, 'And even when I did, I was hopeless. There is no way I'll be able to keep up with all these normal people. When the trainer comes in, I'll ask for a quiet word so I can fill him in on my unique situation. I'm obviously going to be a special case.'

Derek

'I hope I get the opportunity to speak with the trainer privately before the session starts,' Derek thought. 'I know I'll be far more educated than the other participants. All my years and experience in senior management – I've got so much to offer these people. It seems crazy to have to 're-train' like this. But I guess I'll play this silly game and go along for the ride.'

Derek wasn't an arrogant man. In fact, he was a humble soul who genuinely liked to help people. Now retired, the 62-year-old wanted to give back to the community by volunteering for not-for-profit humanitarian organisations. He knew that they'd benefit from his 40-plus years of study and workplace experience.

Was it really three months now? To Derek it seemed more like three weeks ago. He'd sat through the endless farewell speeches from his colleagues. One after another they praised his tireless dedication to the role and the company. Then he was presented with a golf bag and a half dozen golf balls that he knew he'd never use. Once, foolishly, Derek had told a colleague that he might take up golf when he retires. Loose words to shadow loose self-promises.

Over the last few weeks, Derek had stared aimlessly at the walls of his harbourside home. After he'd left his office for the last time, he began to feel lost – even empty – after so many years of meaningful work. 'What I'm missing,' Derek thought, 'is contributing. What I've lost, is this feeling of … worth.'

It had occurred to Derek that he might reclaim some of his sense of purpose if he could volunteer to help others. He could pass on the wealth of his knowledge to them. But Derek was told that in order to achieve this, he would need to re-train; he'd need to attend a vocational education organisation to be certified. Even the thought of attending such a place was humiliating. 'After all my years of experience I have to stoop to this level? This is so … beneath me.' But Derek now accepted that to reach his new goals, re-training was mandatory.

In order to cope with the embarrassment and – let's face it – the indignity of joining a class of amateurs, Derek convinced himself that throughout the classes he'd help both the other participants and the trainer. 'I'll be like a second trainer,' he thought. 'Some of the time I'll even train the trainer.'

Derek knew exactly what he'd wear to the first training session. Despite advice from his wife, he donned the very same suit he wore to his last day of work. Brenda tried to talk him out of this.

'You'll look foolish if you out-dress the other participants,' she said, 'let alone the trainer.'

The couple compromised with Derek choosing the suit but only carrying the jacket. The paisley tie, on the other hand, was staying firmly anchored by a perfect Windsor Knot. Walking out the door, he glanced at his reflection in the hallway mirror. 'Yes,' he said to himself. 'You've still got it, Young Derek.'

Derek grabbed his briefcase, placed it on the back seat of his BMW, carefully placed his suit coat on the back seat hanger, and set off towards the training facility. A few blocks from the centre he found a parking spot and decided that the walk would do him good.

Arriving twenty minutes early at the Registered Training Organisation's office, Derek asked the receptionist if he could speak with the trainer before the session started. The receptionist explained that the trainer usually doesn't have much time between his arrival and commencement of the session. Derek let out a disappointed breath and headed upstairs to the classroom. He stopped at the doorway to study the empty room, eventually selecting a seat in the middle of the horseshoe-configured tables. While he waited, he scanned his phone, re-reading old workplace emails long ago answered.

'When the trainer comes in, I'll ask for a quiet word so I can fill him in on my situation. I'm obviously going to be a special case.'

Liam

The salt water was still running down his body as he dropped his board and picked up his towel. The surf was particularly good this morning. Good surf was the only thing that would get Liam out of bed before 11 am.

At eighteen, high school seemed a distant and dreaded memory for Liam, even though it was less than two years ago. The regimented routine didn't suit him in any way. He fought with the teachers, admin staff and most of his fellow students. He fell into a group of like-minded friends that led him on many negative and destructive paths. For Liam, scholastic failure was the rule rather than the exception and by the time he was forced to leave school it was the expected. This led his immediate family to nag and push him in directions they thought he should go. This however, wasn't the biggest kick in the teeth from his family.

It was after one particular family argument where it seemed a switch was flipped. His family stopped pushing, stopped nagging and even stopped encouraging. They just gave up. No more aggressive 'get out of bed', 'get a job', 'join the army', 'Why can you be more like your brother?' Just nothing. Liam just existed. He felt he was sponging off his parents. He had no money to socialise with his apathetic friends let alone rent his own place away from the guilt he felt at home.

It was only this morning that Liam decided to turn up for a course at the local Registered Training Organisation, more to appease his mother and turn the relationship switch back on than anything else. However, the surf always came first.

He grabbed his board and made his way to the surf club's outdoor shower. He rinsed off, soaking his semi-dry clothes as he put them on, reasoning that the four-block walk would give the early morning sun ample time to dry everything off before he reached the training room.

His walk began briskly with keenness driving his legs up a steep incline. Keenness that was rooted in the hope of some sort of new beginning, whatever that would be, and reconciliation or whatever you would call it with his family.

As he thought of new possibilities, he was bombarded by old fears and self-doubts. 'I'm not good enough, I've always failed, I will be made fun of again, I'll be the youngest one in the class, I'll feel stupid.'

As these negative thoughts engulfed him, his steps slowed and the surfboard he was carrying became heavier and heavier. With shoulders slouched he considered walking the other direction home or to his usual refuge, back to the beach to sit on the comforting sand. Liam sat on a red brick fence to gather his thoughts. Leaning his board against the fence he thought, 'What if they make fun of me and the way I look or dress?'

CHAPTER 1 ~ FELICITY

He looked out from where he was sitting at two parked cars. One a brand-new BMW, the other a beat up old … well, he wasn't sure what it was but he knew it was probably older than him. These cars reminded him of the nagging from his parents. 'What do you want to do with your life? Where are you headed?'

'Do I want the way things had been or do I want a brand-new shiny direction leading to a potentially prosperous life?' he wondered.

It was with great hesitancy that Liam rose to his feet, but it was with renewed determination that he strode down the last two blocks to the training venue.

Liam walked inside the building, asked the receptionist which training room his session was in and leaned his surfboard against the wall next to the courtesy coffee machine. He stood in the doorway, surveying the classroom, and decided to sit next to a girl about his age who didn't acknowledge him other than shifting her chair slightly away, giving him more room. He draped his wet towel over the seat behind him and thought he would like to speak to the trainer before the session started. It was too late, as the session had already begun.

'I wasn't that late,' Liam thought, 'only half an hour. I'll have to ask someone for a spare pen and paper. When the trainer gets a chance, I'll ask for a quiet word so I can fill him in on my situation. I'm obviously going to be a special case.'

Felicity

'I'll wear long sleeves today,' Felicity thought as she selected the colour and style of top and skirt she would wear. 'Skirt!' she thought. 'School was the last time I wore a skirt.'

Long sleeves were a good decision for at least this first day of her new adventure. It would not only hide her ever expanding gallery of tattoos but also her old and some new scars. She was used to people judging her at first site on her tattoos but didn't want the condemnation or judgment of her mental health issues. The thick black stockings covered her pale legs so that was never going to be a problem. Staring in the mirror, she decided that removing any of the multitude of piercings that adorned her face was just too much trouble. Anyway, some things she didn't want to hide. The people that would think she was 'loopy' were the same people she didn't wish to deal with.

Felicity currently works at a convenience store. A job she enjoys. It was her fourth job since leaving school but this one paid more money and had Trudy, her new best friend. This made it all the harder to leave now that she had made the decision to undertake further training. The first training she had undertaken since leaving school six years ago at fourteen.

As Felicity applied the usual copious amounts of makeup that covered her already beautiful face, she recalled the other jobs she had. The first one was as a Nanny to a rich family. She loved working with young Aiden and his mother. She only met the father once as he was always overseas on business. The problem was the parents had constantly tried to save her, as did a lot of the middle-aged men in her next job. She quickly moved on to thinking about her brief stint at the petrol station, which led her to meet Trudy and eventually brought them both to the convenience store.

Felicity felt a little guilty at having to leave that job but there was no way Mr Sing would allow her to dominate the evening roster, freeing her for a four day a week course. Anyway, she looked forward to seeing Trudy in their lunch breaks and regular nights out.

As Felicity descended the stairs from her tiny one-bedroom flat, she hoped that everything she needed would be in the huge duffle bag draped over her shoulder. She brought pens and paper even though she was certain they would be supplied. She thought of how she would be able to have long lunches with Trudy and leave early to prepare for her regular night time sojourns. Felicity had no problem telling white lies to get what she wanted. After all, it's her life and most establishment rules were not meant for her. 'When the trainer comes in, I'll ask for a quiet word so I can fill him in on my situation. I'm obviously going to be a special case.'

Amy

Amy was absolutely petrified as her mother wheeled her chair to the back of the taxi cab, waiting for the driver to lower the ramp.

This was a routine procedure since Amy's diagnosis, but today was the first day she would be attending a course on her own with able-bodied classmates all staring at the crumpled freak in the motorised wheelchair. Her mother never pushed her to do anything she didn't want to do. A lesson learned long ago when she aggressively encouraged Amy to see the myriad of specialists who claimed a miracle cure, only to be told in no uncertain terms by her daughter, 'No more useless snake oil salesmen.'

For a while now, Amy had accepted her lot in life and had been content on being at home watching TV and doing her beloved jigsaw puzzles. Her once many friends had trickled down to just a handful – in her case a handful meant two or maybe three if you count her ex-boyfriend Jake, who hung around cautiously through obligation and guilt. They had both agreed to cease their romantic relationship as it was a logical progression of the circumstances. Though Amy couldn't help but feel the downgrade of their relationship was more Jake's deliberate deconstruction rather than a mutually accepted and agreed to progression.

Enrolling in the course was for two reasons: one, so she and Mum could have some much needed time away from each other, and two, a deep-seated desire to meet new people and possibly make new friends and maybe even learn something on the way.

As the rear door of the cab shut, Amy gave a cursory wave to her mother, who showed no intention of moving from the sidewalk until the taxicab had rounded the corner out of sight. The cab driver wanted to chat about the Paralympics and his friend missing a leg, but Amy was not in the mood. She answered with single words or grunts. Halfway to the drop off, the cab driver gave up his attempts and they travelled in silence the rest of the way.

The helpful office girl came down the flight of stairs to help Amy enter the stair lift. As the chair slowly made its short but slow journey, two people passed her, squeezing around the chair lift. One of the passers-by even carried a surfboard with him and negotiated the narrow space by placing the fibreglass plank on his head. Amy noticed that this young guy was the only one to acknowledge her as she ascended the rest of the way.

As the small gate raised so she could leave the platform, Amy thought, 'When the trainer gets a chance, I'll ask for a quiet word so I can fill him in on my situation. I'm obviously going to be a special case.'

Miranda

The main reason Miranda left the boutique was not because the organisation's owner was a 'trailer trash cow', or that the owner's daughter 'wouldn't know good fashion if it bit her on her ample backside'. It was because she knew that she could do better. They never appreciated her and what she offered the organisation anyway.

Leaving the store was much easier than she thought. Miranda was a little surprised at how well Meg, the owner, took the news she had decided to leave. Strangely she seemed almost pleased, however, that couldn't be the case as Meg knew how important she was to the upmarket store. Libby, the daughter, gave her two air kisses as she left for the last time, promising to catch up at some time. Miranda agreed but also knew this would never happen.

Miranda thought of this as she was finishing off her morning ritual of applying perfect makeup on her perfect facial features. This procedure usually took a good hour, with hair adding another half hour at least. Makeup was a strategic art form and required subtle adjustments to suit different situations, and starting an adult education course was definitely a subtle adjustment.

Miranda was not nervous at all. Confidence was never a lacking attribute as she was growing up. As an only child, she seemed to always be the centre of attention at home and she made sure that was the case at school. She could do no wrong by her parents, excelling at everything in their eyes. This was the catalyst for some difficulties at school, in

CHAPTER 1 ~ MIRANDA

particular high school, where even though she was challenged by teachers and other students, she still accepted that she was exceptional and her limited friends and poor grades were other people's prejudices and jealousies, not her problem. They could just talk to the hand.

Her close friends – well, her only friends – were Skye, who went with her to Paris a couple of summers ago, Trudy, Amanda and Tyler, their gay friend. Having Tyler as part of their 'rat pack', as they called themselves, gave their little tribe a sense of worldly acceptance.

They were all wonderful people, so they thought. In fact, for an hour on Christmas Eve they would sing Carols at the local Children's Hospital. 'Sing' was probably being too generous, as it was more like a giggling, laughing mess. Probably due to the shots Trudy made them have just before they left to perform this community service sacrifice. They were sure that the kids loved it, but they were usually escorted prematurely from the building. It was the thought that counted, right?

Miranda didn't have to think about what she would wear today, as she was a natural fashionista. She was now a professional and all she had to do was decide on the bag to take. A quick peruse of the spare room-come-wardrobe yielded results.

'Perfect!' she exclaimed as she grabbed a bag with a long strap that draped comfortably over her shoulder. Before leaving her room, she took one long look in the mirror and headed down the few stairs to the street.

On the three-block walk to the training venue, Miranda passed a shining BMW, a glistening reminder her of her goals and aspirations. In stark contrast, the pathetic, crying woman seated alone in the wreck of a car parked immediately behind the BMW reminded her of what she was determined not to become.

Now in an oddly pensive mood, Miranda, just for a moment came out of her well-constructed fantasy and recalled her reality.

She was desperately lonely growing up. Brenda, her imaginary friend morphed in response to Miranda's age. At first, she was a fairy who could do wonderful magic, then she became the sister Miranda never had, and finally a travel agent that planned wonderful journeys away from the constant fighting and yelling at home. Though upon reaching school, two major events happened for Miranda. The first one, mysteriously overnight, Brenda disappeared. The next was when her dad left her mum and the family home. For a while, peace and serenity was the unfamiliar norm. Then her mother started to drink more and more, and this aligned with Miranda not doing anything right at home or at school. The yelling continued but no longer at her father; it was all focused on her. 'I had to leave,' Miranda thought. She got a job after school to help pay for her being able to go with the rest of her French class to Paris.

Miranda was so tired at school; she couldn't keep up with her classes or her grades and very quickly she fell behind. After her frugal trip to Paris it was obvious that she would have to leave both school and home. That's when Aunty Meg offered her a job on Thursday nights and Saturday mornings. Her cousin Libby also worked there and would show her the ropes. She was at first worried about working with the daughter of the boss, concerned Meg would show favouritism. But they never had much to say to each other and Meg treated them the same anyway. This made life easy for Miranda but Libby was unimpressed and made her feelings privately and publicly known. Miranda had wondered whether she should ring her mum, tell her what she was doing. She never had, certain Meg would have filled her in by now with sarcastic twists showing her disdain. Miranda was only in the last fortnight back on speaking terms with her Mother and speaking only before her Mother's liquid 'self-medication' reabsorbed her into her numb fantasy world.

Miranda shook her head and quickened her pace as she snapped out of her true reality and reabsorbed herself into her well-constructed persona.

She would need to leave the class early some days or arrive late depending on photo shoot scheduling. Sometimes she may have to leave at a moment's notice when her agent texts her. This is why she will have to have her mobile phone with her and on at all times.

Of course, there were no modelling contracts and no agent.

'When the trainer gets a chance, I'll ask for a quiet word so I can fill him in on my unique situation. I'm obviously going to be a special case.'

Ricky

'Will I put all my pens in my bag or just the ones people have given me over the years? I like pens.'

'Richard' is how his father addresses him, but Ricky caused less problems at school and at the support centre when people called him 'Ricky'. His mother had left them when Ricky was four or five, but he does remember her calling him Ricky. Maybe that is where he got it from.

Mum 'couldn't take it anymore and deserved better and anyway we would be much better off without her.' This was a firm milestone in Ricky's memory. Growing up, he was always told that he must miss her terribly, but Ricky wasn't sure if he missed her or not. After so many people telling him how much he must miss her, he realised that he better play along and say yes and even squeeze out a few crocodile tears for added conviction.

Ricky couldn't read facial expressions very well, so he listened to words but sometimes words have more than one meaning and even then, words don't align with expressions, meanings, emotions or agendas. It was easier to hide in his room painting, drawing or reading than dealing with these 'word shadows'. Ricky would often sit alone in the quiet sanctuary of his room rocking forward and back, forward and back while reading, drawing or just thinking. He didn't like TV. The flickering hurt his eyes. He did like certain cartoons and commercials, but those were few and far between. At least on his computer he could create his own entertainment, not be 'force fed' someone else's shallow meaningless projections.

Ricky was worried about this training, as there are so many things he must concentrate on *not* doing. I must not talk too much or at the wrong times. I must not tell people that they are wrong, especially in front of people and especially the trainer. I must not rock back and forward during class because people stare at me. I'm generally not good with other people however the truth is, other people are not very good with me.

At school Ricky had very few friends. After many rejections Ricky found it far more comfortable to be alone. He didn't mind. It made it much easier for him to get lost in his own thoughts of complex theories, logic and reasoning, sometimes dealing with numbers and geometrics and occasionally his personal philosophies. It was during these times that class bullies would ply their ruthless trade on him. Sometimes it was simple and prolonged physical abuse but mostly verbal taunts and ridicule. For the most part Ricky ignored their jibes and annoying slaps. Any retaliation was always in his mind where he was author of some amazing, quick-witted retorts. Except for this one time where Craig Anderson kept slapping his face, seeking a reaction. This time Ricky's nonverbal response had no effect and after twenty-three slaps against the left cheek, Ricky reacted. Before getting to his feet, Ricky punched Craig under the chin.

He later found out that he had 'a prime uppercut'. Well at least that's what his father told him. Craig stumbled backwards and fell to the ground with a startled look. Ricky grabbed a nearby steel garbage bin that adorned every country school playground and smashed it against Craig's face. The steel lid flew off and paper, orange and banana peel and empty drink bottles exploded outward. Craig was letting out a muffled scream but at least the slapping had stopped. Ricky was watching from afar as his own arms brought the steel bin down upon Craig's head again and again. Eventually Craig had stopped making that annoying noise just as two teachers tackled Ricky to the concrete, sending the severely dented bin rolling across the playground.

As Ricky passively submitted to the teachers, he felt obligated to tell them that he had incapacitated Craig Anderson. He's not hitting or abusing anyone anymore. 'I fixed a problem. You don't have to punish him and by the way, why are you holding me down? I'm the hero.'

Craig came back to school two months later but had lost a lot of weight as for six weeks he had to eat through a straw. Most of the bruising had faded but he didn't look at Ricky on that first day back as they passed each other in a hallway. This made it difficult as Ricky had been instructed to apologise to Craig by his Counsellor. Even the police didn't grasp Ricky's reasoning even though it was simple Newtonian logic. 'Craig was hitting me and yelling abuse at me. I made him stop.' Simple. That didn't stop Ricky having to do six months of volunteer work at the local Salvation Army sorting clothes.

Ricky recalled all these things as he walked the six or so blocks to the training room. This past incident reminded him of two primary fears he had carried with him through life – well at least since school. The first was that he hoped that there will be no people like Craig Anderson in his class. The second, he hoped the classroom had plastic garbage bins.

'When the trainer gets a chance, I'll ask for a quiet word so I can fill him in on my situation. I'm obviously going to be a special case.'

Alistair

Alistair placed his hand-crafted leather briefcase on the desk at the front of the classroom. He had only been to this room twice before, and then only for short two-hour seminars on communication in the workplace.

He took a minute to reflect before the participants arrived on how he got there. What brought him to this point in his life.

Al was a library kid at school. During lunchbreaks, recess and whenever he was able to produce a doctor's certificate allowing him to avoid PE, he would seek refuge in the library. After leaving school he got an apprenticeship with a large accountancy firm. After 30 years with the same organisation, the now faltering company called to volunteer redundancy for senior staff. Alistair was hesitant, as he was addicted to stable, unfaltering routine of his life. Pressure and corporate writing on the wall dictated the inevitable, so he decided to take the very handsome redundancy package as well as the sizeable superannuation amount, he had accumulated over 30 years.

Money was not the problem. Shrewd investments meant that even if he never had another paying job, he would still be financially well-off for the rest of his life. The problem was working was all he had. A bachelor by choice and aversion to socialising meant that at almost 50, Al had an intrenched routine that focused on nobody else but himself. What would he do with an extra 12 hours a day that was allocated to his work life?

Online he spotted an ad in the local community news that stated an organisation was seeking out experienced individuals who were qualified in their field of expertise that would be prepared to share their knowledge and practical experience to others through a Registered Training Organisation.

Alistair had never been a social or even a personable individual. However, at this juncture in his life, common sense told him a new venture may be just what is needed. Although this was an exciting thought, it was also a terrifying one as he contemplated a myriad of negative and humiliating scenarios.

He had attended all the trainer briefing sessions and even acquired all the mandatory online qualifications needed to deliver a course. He had chosen and was advised to deliver sessions on workplace interpersonal skills and human resource management.

On paper, Alistair was an ideal presenter, with three decades of practical experience and every relevant and specific qualification imaginable. The problem that haunted him was the crucial fact that he didn't like people. He had a fundamental aversion to others. People frustrated him, they bewildered him. It's not that he had a sense of superiority; it's just that he found difficulty in communicating with, listening to and advising others. 'What if what I told them was wrong?'

Alistair had always been lacking in self-awareness and confidence. However, this new trainer venture, although out of his comfort zone, is what he needed. Simmering under the surface he feared having to talk to others about non-course-related issues. As he looked out on a still empty training room, mentally preparing for the first day of his course, he pondered fearfully if the participants he hadn't met yet wanted to tell him their own sob stories and seek special consideration because they feel they are a 'special case'.

Chapter 2

Andragogy and Vocational Education

Since andragogy and pedagogy are two teaching methods that are very popular, it is helpful to know the difference between the two. Andragogy is the practice of observing and studying adult learning methodologies, whereas pedagogy is the traditional method of teaching, generally applied to children. These concepts have developed and evolved over the millennium. Though there are some similarities in adult and children learning, there are many differences and substantial variations that need to be highlighted for those who are involved with such studies. Therefore, this section of the chapter presents to you the difference between pedagogy and andragogy.

The definition of pedagogy is simply the method and practice of delivering education material and all it encompasses. Pedagogy refers to the way educators deliver the content of a subject, topic or course curriculum to participants usually children.

The methods used to help adults learn concepts or practical applications are different to the methods that are used to help children learn. Methodologies and philosophies that focus on adults and are concerned with helping them learn more effectively and efficiently form the basis of andragogy. The information based upon knowledge and experience is presented in a form more conducive to adult learning. For example, peer review through seminars and workshops.

There are some fundamental assumptions that form the backbone of adult learning. For example, there is an assumption that adults are more interested in learning concepts that are relevant to their work and personal lives through practical application. To some extent this is true. Adults require innate or internal motivators rather than external ones. Learning new concepts requires practical experience that also includes errors, correction and in some cases, a form of discipline. Additionally, adults can be more responsible than children in monitoring their evaluation through self-assessment and self-awareness.

To summarise the Oxford dictionary states, andragogy is 'The method and practice of teaching adult learners; adult education.'

The *Encyclopedia Britannica* defines vocational education as 'instruction intended to equip persons for industrial or commercial occupations. It may be obtained either formally in trade schools, technical secondary schools, or in on-the-job training programs or, more informally, by picking up the necessary skills on the job' *(Update: March 21, 2024, https: www.britannica.com/topic/vocational-education)*. This definition makes it clear that vocational education is not a new area of learning.

Vocational Education in Schools

Vocational education in schools is a relatively modern development. Until the 19th century, vocational education was provided only by apprenticeship, traineeships or on the job training at respective professions. This situation was in part due to the low social status associated with such education as opposed to a scholastic or academic curriculum, which was considered necessary for a gentleman of class. With the growth of industrialisation during the 19th century, several European countries, notably Germany, began introducing vocational education in elementary and secondary schools. In Great Britain, opposition to vocational education persisted into the 20th century, aligning with post industrial age philosophies and mandates and a war period that included the First and Second World Wars. Despite this, a few trade and junior technical schools were established by local authorities prior to the commencement of World War II.

By the late 19th century, public school vocational education consisted of manual training and practical applications. These programs were slowly expanded until 1917, when government aid was provided to public schools for trade, industrial, agricultural, and homemaking studies.

Upon the conclusion of World War II, the demand for trained adults in the relatively new fields of computer science, electronics and medical services led to an increased demand for short-term postsecondary specialised training programs as an alternative to a traditional college education.

Adult Education

Adult education, or continuing education, is any form of learning undertaken by or provided for mature men and women.

As found in *Encyclopedia Britannica,* A 1970 report, from the National Institute of Adult Education (England and Wales) defined adult education as 'any kind of education for people who are old enough to work, vote, fight and marry and who have completed the cycle of continuous education, [if any] commenced in childhood' Adult education has such diverse modes as independent study consciously supported with or without the aid of libraries; broadcast programs or correspondence courses; group discussion and other 'mutual aid' learning in study circles, colloquia, seminars, workshops, tutorial and Information Technology sessions.' (1970).

Simply put, vocational education and training (VET) is designed to impart specific workplace related skills and knowledge. VET covers a wide range of careers and industries, including trade and office work, retail, hospitality, tourism, health care, leadership and management, education, technology, disabilities, plus many more.

Another form of adult education is nonvocational, which relates to learning that is not directly linked to workplace learning. This can include hobbies, life skills, interests and volunteer placement duties in various community and non-community areas. This does not mean that the skills possessed for undertaking non-workplace activities cannot be used or even acquired in or from the workplace. However, staff development through vocational education is generally specific to the individual's roles and responsibilities within that individual's workplace. Therefore, workplace learned skills and nonvocational skills can be of great benefit to vocational and the nonvocational sectors.

The fundamental basis of education is the transference of knowledge, skills, aptitude and understanding in a particular area of need or want. This cognitive transfer can be undertaken through many mediums such as face to face, coaching, mentoring, online, seminars, workshops or sitting by a campfire listening to someone of experience relay 'how they did it in the old days'. It's like watching someone tie a knot that holds a boat to its mooring.

Chapter 3

Who Should be a Vocational or Adult Educator?

It is important at the outset of this chapter to emphatically state that not all people can or should be adult workplace educators.

In the majority of cases when an adult educator is created, people just don't manifest as a ready-to-go, all-encompassing trainer/facilitator. It takes years of trial and error as well as personal and professional behaviour adjustments and constant vigilance and redevelopment, which includes study and research.

The three fundamental criteria for a vocational educator are as follows:

1. Knowledge
2. Experience
3. The ability to effectively communicate

A trainer must know their topic intimately. They must have firsthand knowledge of the topic or subject to be delivered. They gain this knowledge through their own training and workplace experience and should be proficient in all areas to be taught. It is also imperative that the trainer constantly updates their knowledge, skills and hands on experience. This acquiring of vocational currency is paramount in presenting both the training organisation and the trainer in the highest professional way. This currency will often include a mandatory accreditation requirement to be able to deliver training.

Practical experience is acquired through hands on workplace activity over a period of time. The prospective trainer must have full understanding of the task or topic from both a practical and theoretical perspective. The experience should include the learned ability to problem solve and the development of strategies to identify issues and implement necessary changes regarding workplace application of a topic or subject.

Ultimately, it doesn't matter how much knowledge of a topic or related practical experience a person has if they do not have knowledge transfer skills. The ability to communicate knowledge and experience to an individual or group of people outside or inside the workplace is the most important element of being a vocational educator. This is where a lot of well-intentioned adult educators fail. It's where the rubber hits the road in face-to-face education. I have seen well educated, exceptionally skilled and experienced individuals falter in front of a class because of their inability to transfer years of acquired knowledge, skills and experience to a group of eager participants. They froze or the message they were trying to deliver drowned in incoherent gibberish. This left them dazed, confused and unable to reconcile this initial sense of failure. Some never returned for a second try at delivering a session. This is a great shame, as with some simple delivery tools these individuals may have become a great vocational educators.

An effective vocational educator does not have to be a great orator or a proficient speech-maker. In fact, in some circumstances it's probably better if they are not. The simple fact is this: A vocational educator must effectively present knowledge of a topic to those who have limited or no knowledge of that topic, in such a way that the information can be accepted, processed, retained, recalled and applied by the participant.

Personal attributes of a vocational trainer include: being able to relate to others, sometimes to individuals or in a group environment, and at other times in front of a huge conference of participants; the ability to focus on the task at hand when there could be huge distractions within the training environment; to be able to project their voice towards the participant that is furthest away; to possess patience and understanding; to have the time to research a topic and retain industry and academic currency; to have the time to do marking and the Registered Training Organisation (RTO)'s required compliance paperwork.

In vocational education, andragogy is the act of teaching adults in, from or about a workplace environment. The theories of andragogy increasingly identify the student or participant as an agent, and the teacher as a facilitator. Conventional western pedagogies, however, view the teacher/facilitator as knowledge/experience holder and student/participant as the recipient of knowledge. Fundamentally in pedagogy, knowledge is given, whereas in andragogy, the gaining of knowledge is sought after as a collaborative effort between facilitator and participant.

When a facilitator plans a presentation, they should consider the different ways that the information can be presented to the participants. Never commence facilitating an education program with a predetermined idea of how you would like your delivery style to be. There are many factors that determine an individual's delivery style including:

- Audience/Participants
- Subject or Course
- Demographics
- Level of understanding

Your style of delivery may change to suite these variations.

Delivery Style

What is a delivery style? There are many factors that determine an individual facilitator's delivery style. These include:

- Personality
- Character
- Temperament
- Previously developed individual delivery preferences
- Experience
- Education to be delivered
- Age and demographics of participants

- Topic to be presented
- Specific and contextual environments
- Organisation delivering the training (RTO)
- Delivery within macro and micro learning environments

All these factors can influence andragogical practices that a facilitator can choose to use.

Facilitators/Trainers may use experience and research from many different formal academic and non-formal experiential areas to help formulate their delivery style decisions and content. For example, a workplace-based facilitator may draw upon leadership skills that they have acquired in a particular workplace role and use those learned or innate skills as a foundation for their own individual educational delivery styles.

The justifications behind the delivery style decisions will form andragogical principles, and every facilitator/trainer will develop their own principles over a continuing and developing time period.

Pedagogical Approaches

The most recognised approaches to pedagogical education are broken down into four categories: behaviourism, constructivism, social constructivism, and liberationist.

Behaviourism

A behaviourist pedagogy uses the theory of Behaviourism to guide its approach. A Behaviourist pedagogical approach means that learning is facilitator-centred, meaning a facilitator should be the sole authority figure in that learning environment and lead the education session. It would advocate the use of direct instruction, and lecture-based presentation.

In the learning/training environment, the theory of Behaviourism came from pedagogical research by Edward Thorndike (1913).

In a session using a Behaviourist pedagogical approach, you may see a mixture of lecturing, modelling and demonstration, rote learning, and choral repetition*. These activities are visible and structured and are led by the facilitator. However, during the session, change may come where the participant is the centre of the activity and demonstrates their topic/subject retention through verbal or visual recall and assessment.

Behaviourism is also sometimes described as a traditional teaching style.

Constructivism

Constructivism is a theory that people learn through experiences and reflection. A Constructivist pedagogy puts the participant at the centre of the learning. This is sometimes called the unseen or 'invisible pedagogy'. A constructivist approach would incorporate project work with questioning-based learning.

Constructivism is based on the pedagogical research of Jean Piaget (1896-1890). Piaget wrote extensively about 'schemas', an idea that the facilitator must present projects and activities to promote learning in parallel with whatever motivation learners come to learn with. In vocational education, projects and activities may be used to support a learning program through symbolic and abstract ideas.

A lesson might include individualisation, a slower pace with unpredictable outcomes. An industry expert shares their personally acquired knowledge and skills by way of practical examples and observation with less facilitator talk. This ideally should align with desired learning outcomes and competency-based results. Some adopters of this pedagogy would also place emphasis on being outdoors and engaging with nature or outdoor industries, such as Primary Industries, landscaping or other outdoor-based trade skills.

Constructivism is also sometimes described as a 'progressive' delivery style.

Social Constructivism

A Social Constructivism pedagogy could be considered a blend of two priorities: facilitator-guided and participant-centred. Cognitive psychologist Lev Vygotsky developed social constructivism believing that learning was a collaborative process between participant and facilitator (1978).

The facilitator would use group work elements, but would include smaller group sizes, and limit the choice in topics or subjects. The use of facilitator modelling, questioning, and a mixture of individual, pair, and all participants instruction was used.

Liberationism

Liberationism is a critical pedagogy developed by the Brazilian educator, Paulo Freire. Freire was the Director of the Pernambuco Department of Education and Culture, and developed an approach of teaching where he was able to teach illiterate adults to read in just forty-five days. Freire focussed on removing the two major barriers to learning: poverty and hunger. Once he was released by the Brazilian military government after a 70-day imprisonment, he wrote a book called *Pedagogy of the Oppressed* (1970), in which he wrote about the dehumanisation of students and argued for cooperation and unity between governing bodies and educators. A Liberationist approach is one where the participant's voice is placed at the centre, and a general democracy is constructed within the learning area. Value is placed on having the facilitator as a learner and the class discovering topics or subjects together.

The facilitator might use examples of literature that contain non-standard constructions, such as parallel relevant example. Students may take on the role of the facilitator and decide upon the topic to be presented. The facilitator should provide space and opportunity for the participant to showcase their learning, and this can take many forms like roleplay, audio visual presentations or relevant demonstration.

Principles of Adult Learning

Andragogy and its adult learning theories have expanded to include an array of principles since 1980, when educator Malcolm Knowles (1984) introduced the concept of andragogy. His six principles of adult learning include:

1. Need to know
2. Experience
3. Self-Concept
4. Readiness to Learn
5. Problem-Centred Approach
6. Intrinsic Motivation

Andragogy makes the following assumptions about the design of learning. These four areas of andragogy are learner focussed and the basis of adult and vocational education:

1. Adults need to know why they need to learn something

Adults need to know what the driving force behind the requirement is to obtain more practical or theoretical knowledge or skills. It could be for personal betterment in the workplace, which could in turn lead to increased fiscal gain or to rise in hierarchical order.

It could go outside a personal will or desire and be an instruction from management, supervisors or a court or other legal directive as a form or correction or discipline.

2. Adults need to learn experientially

Years of an individual's existence equates directly to experience and knowledge gain. For a variety of reasons, an individual may determine that they either need or would like to obtain more knowledge and experience for personal or professional betterment. Observation and practical instruction is a primary method for an adult individual to learn.

'To hear someone is to listen. To see someone is to understand.'

David W. Mayne

3. Adults approach learning as problem-solving

If an adult is faced with a professional or personal issue, the observation or interpretation from someone who has knowledge or experience relating directly to that same issue may give great understanding and insight towards a resolution. A different perspective from someone who has had similar issues but addressed from a different perspective may shine new light and perspective on your own issue.

4. Adults learn best when the topic is of immediate value

If the participant is motivated by professional, personal development progression, need or directive, when a person's motivation for seeking out vocational learning is clear, the will and inclination for the participant to devote considerable time and dedication to the learning process will follow.

Adults need to know that the knowledge and skills required will be of immediate benefit to them as an individual.

Chapter 4

Verbal and Nonverbal Communication for Observational Research and as an Educational Training Resource

'What we hear from others is important however what we see in others is vital.'

David W. Mayne

Communication is crucial when dealing with others. It helps us gain better understanding and therefore meaning and intent. This is important in any adult learning environment. You are often dealing with many people at one time and each of those individuals present their own unique way of communicating with others.

As an educator/trainer/facilitator you are primarily a communicator. You are transferring knowledge and practical skills to another person and ascertaining through observation and verbal communication if that information has been received, understood and retained.

Effective communication is imperative to success in any learning environment. It could be the difference between a pass or a fail. It could have very little to do with an individual's cognitive ability but more to do with that individual's primary method of communication and how effective it is. Holistic communication can also lessen misunderstandings and potential escalated conflict situations. Therefore, it is important for a facilitator/trainer to possess even some rudimentary interpretative communication skills.

All living creatures communicate in some form. It could be a dog wagging its tail or bearing its teeth, or a bee doing a dance at the front of its hive to indicate to other worker bees a pollen or nectar source. Professor Satoshi Sawai at the University of Tokyo has even identified that single cell amoebas can communicate with other amoebas.

Different countries and cultures have different communication variations, both verbal and nonverbal. As individuals, there may be a myriad of communication variations brought about by parent or sibling influences during our formative years, or through our own determinations made through observation and experience. Due to some form of cognitive impairment, there may also be other variations to how a person communicates with others. Therefore, it is easy to understand how difficult it is in some situations to accurately and effectively understand meaning through the communication presented by some individuals.

In the learning environment the facilitator should take on the role as novice profiler. Subtly observe the speech and body language of participants to ascertain the best and most effective way of communicating with them. Also try to determine any potential communication variations needed due to possible cognitive or physical impairment. Acquiring the skills for holistic communication goes a long way to becoming a effective adult educator or educator.

Verbal Communication

Verbal Communication is a type of oral communication wherein the message is transmitted through spoken words. Here the sender gives words to their feelings, thoughts, ideas and opinions and expresses them in the form of speeches, discussions, presentations, and conversations.

It's not only what is said that is important, but also how it is said. Words are the template of communication; however, distortion and misunderstanding can arise from the other related factors around our speech. These include:

- Volume
- Tone
- Pace
- Inflection
- Accent
- Impediments

Volume

Volume ensures that we are heard or that we can hear what's being said. However, if the volume does not align or compliment with what's being said then people may interpret your message differently to how you wish to present it.

A softer, slower voice when presenting a topic may give poignancy and emphasis to the topic being delivered. This can be a very effective teaching tool utilizing the contrast effect. The contrast effect is where variation to the normal volume or tone of a facilitator's delivery varies enough to grab the attention of the participant and make them aware of the point being presented. It may also jolt them from a state of lethargy if the topic presented is of little or no interest to the participant.

At times it is this variation to the trainer's normal 'baseline' tone and volume of delivery that brings back the participants interest in what is verbally being presented. Conversely, a harder and louder change of voice tone and volume may have the same effect of gaining the attention of an individual or an entire class but in an adverse, negative way. A louder voice is often received as a sign of aggression or discipline. Once participants are familiar with a trainer, a rise in volume can be received as an excellent way of emphasising a certain point or ensuring that all participants are attentive to what is being said or about to be said. For example, when the facilitator is presenting to a group of participants an important issue regarding health and safety procedures that may have potential mortality consequences and needs to be emphasised as critically important information.

Tone

'Your voice expresses your personality, and your tone portrays your mood.'

– David W Mayne

In presenting information, tone can be used to emphasise a point or an entire topic to an individual or group of participants.

If your tone is inconsistent and variable, participants will notice. For example, if you speak in a professional academic tone in your presentation, then change suddenly to a more relaxed tone full of inferences and colloquial dialogue. This inconsistency can make participants uncomfortable and can make them less likely to trust the information that you are presenting or trust you as the presenter.

An example of how tone can influence the speaker's intent is the phrase 'yeah right'. In a certain sentence, this phrase can be heard as demeaning sarcasm. However, if it is said with a lighter tone, it can be heard as positive and affirming.

It is important to be consistent in your tone of speech. Positive and affirming.

Pace

If a presenter speaks to quickly then to an audience, the words may appear distorted or blended together and meaning can be lost. A listener may spend so much time trying to understand quickly spoken words that whole context and understanding of what's being said is missed. A common symptom of a nervous public speaker is adrenalin-induced rapid speech. This is common for those who are new to public speaking or are addressing an unfamiliar audience or who are not confident or competent in delivering a certain topic.

Speaking too quickly is one of the most common speech problems. Perhaps because almost all of us tend to speed up our speech when we are stressed or excited.

When meeting a new class, presenting new or unfamiliar information, or presenting to a potentially hostile audience, it is natural to be nervous. All these situations may be stressful and cause all kinds of physiological responses, including speeding up our speech.

Some people, however, are genuine motormouths. These are people who always speak rapidly and sometimes unnecessarily. Speaking too slowly is much less common, but there are people who tend to speak naturally with a rate of speed that leaves gaps between words and draws out syllables to extremes.

The basic principle for pace when public speaking is to ensure you are speaking at a pace that is clear to the audience and can be understood and information retained. Listening is only part of the process. Once you physically hear what is being said, then you as an individual must convert that into relevance, understanding and therefore meaning. Context is gained and knowledge acquired. This acquisition on knowledge is then confirmed through an individual's recall of the subject matter.

Your speech signature is your baseline of normal presentation pace. It is your own unique method of vocal delivery. This is a fingerprint for your vocalisation. If you speak outside that fingerprint, it may distort and therefore interfere with the whole process of communication.

If you speak too slowly or in a 'staccato' manner, then the listener may have too much time to process what they are actually hearing and may misinterpret what is being said.

It is important for a presenter to keep active observation of those they are presenting to. Note verbal or nonverbal communication that may signal that a participant does not know or understand what is being said. Phrases like 'could you say that again' or a participant displaying a puzzled look may show that the presenter is speaking too quickly for the participant to process and understand.

Slowing Your Speech Down
Concentrating on enunciation when we speak a good way to slow down our speech. When we focus on enunciating clearly, we force ourselves to stop slurring and eliding syllables when we speak.

For better understanding, a presenter may enunciate their words clearly and concentrate on pronunciation and phrasing. Verbal punctuation is also important when presenting. For example, a listener should equate a pause in dialogue with a full stop. Those presenters that speak quickly will often ignore verbal punctuation and phrasing. Compacting all the sentences can confuse the listener, distorting the intent of the address and therefore causing loss of meaning.

As stated earlier, nerves can be a primary reason for fast-paced speaking. This often adjusts over time and with familiarity with the listeners. Relaxation techniques can help settle the nerves but unless medically prescribed, never take medication or alcohol to mask nervousness, as the potential arises for a false or distorted personality be presented. There is also the potential for words and actions inappropriate for an educational environment to manifest.

For participants that have English as a second language, it is not only a good teaching method but also polite to slow your speech down and enunciate your words clearly. This goes for those that may have some cognitive limitations or physical or intellectual disability.

The best indicator that you are speaking at a suitable pace for a participant or participants is by observation and verbal interactions during your delivery. Observe body language to see if there is a 'quizzical' look on participants faces or repeated questions asking for you to repeat what is being said. If this is a regular occurrence or you suspect it may be, then modify your speech both volume and pace and observe if these bewildered expressions by the participants cease.

Inflection

'How you say something can be more important than what you are actually saying'

– David W. Mayne

Inflection is a crucial part of speaking effectively. Inflection not only gives emphasis to certain words, sentences or phrases but also goes a long way in verbal punctuation that can give clarity, meaning and intent to what is being said. It is important to note that different languages and different cultures employ different meaning to inflection. In some languages inflection can determine urgency and even gender.

There are four types of inflection:

- Rising
- Falling
- Rising circumflex
- Falling circumflex

Rising inflection at the end of a sentence expresses doubt, uncertainty or even questioning. Falling inflection gives authority and an ending to what's being said. Circumflex inflection verbally opposes the down and up inflection patterns. This tells the listener that the speaker has not yet finished their verbal presentation however, is taking a pause but has not yet completed their presentation.

Inflection is an important communication tool and is vital in presenting structure and contexts to a presentation. When a presenter or public speaker exaggerates inflections, it can be used to emphasise a particular point or to present a suspense or dramatic affect.

Punctuation

The correct use of inflection can punctuate a sentence being spoken. As was mentioned earlier, downward inflection on the last word of a sentence can mean the end of a sentence or topic. Upward or rising inflection on the first word of a new sentence signifies the start of a new topic or new sentence. If the speaker or presenter is asking a question or rhetorical statement, then there is an exception to this verbal structure. Upward inflection on the last word of a sentence alerts the listener to a question being asked or a rhetorical statement being made. This may vary from culture to culture or language to language. For example, as in some Asian countries upward or downward inflection is determined by the gender of the person spoken to or about.

Conversational Oscillation Inflection

When we talk to family or acquaintances, we talk with conversational oscillation of speech. The pattern of upward or downward inflection is determined by content, situation and the listener. There is no pre-determined pattern of speech, just a relaxed and well-paced communication of thoughts and ideas that is reciprocated in kind.

This type of communication is relaxed, non-authoritarian and easy to listen to. It puts both presenter and listener at ease and makes them comfortable enough to respond as part of a conversation.

When a facilitator delivers via conversational delivery, it is usually to a small group or to a group of participants that are familiar with the facilitator and feel relaxed with that type of delivery. Other examples where conversational delivery may be beneficial is while mentoring or coaching. Using professional, academic or regimented delivery in a one-on-one coaching or mentoring scenario could create a sense of falseness around the facilitator and make participants feel awkward and uncomfortable.

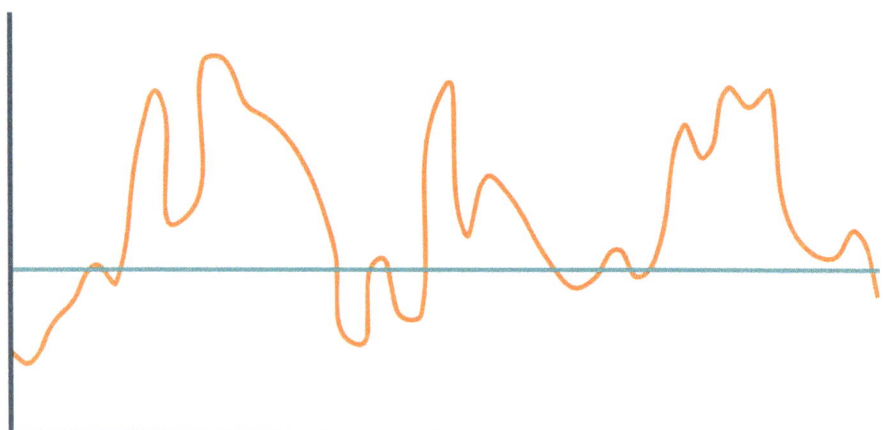

Accent

A facilitator must never assume that all participants in a group have the same level of understanding of the English language. Even those from other countries who speak excellent English may have strong accents that can be difficult to understand, just as the presenter's accent may be difficult to understand for some participants.

It is vital to find a pace and volume of well-enunciated speech that the participant is comfortable with. This can be determined without embarrassment to the participant by observing their expressions to determine understanding of what is being said. If still in doubt, then during a session break ask if you have been understood. If not, ask how you can improve the delivery so that the participant will not miss anything being said in the session.

Impediments

There are many physical, intellectual and cognitive reasons why an individual may not be receptive to what's being said by another individual. Listening is not just receiving the verbal information. It is processing that information and, in the listener's mind, classifying and retaining it.

A hearing disability may severely impinge on a participant's ability to understand what is being presented clearly. If the disability is physical and declared at enrolment, then the participant should sit in a position within the training room that maximizes the clarity of the facilitator's presentation. If the participant has not disclosed their hearing difficulties to the facilitator, the facilitator needs to observe any potential hearing difficulties by watching the participant's body language and verbal interactions with yourself or other participants that may signal an issue. If there is doubt that the participant is not hearing clearly, then privately ask the participant if there is an issue. If confirmed that they are having hearing difficulties, then encourage the participant to move to a location within the training room that will be more conducive to clarity. If the participant refuses to disclose a possible hearing limitation, then there is nothing that the facilitator can do other than be conscious of a possible hearing issue with that participant and make an effort to speak louder and clearer.

The same principles are relevant if the participant has an eyesight problem that may hinder them from observing or reading information that the facilitator has presented as a visual training aid. The visually impaired participant should position themselves within the learning area to maximise visual effectiveness to enhance the learning process.

If a participant's physical impairment requires the use of walking sticks, wheelchairs, crutches or prosthetics, usually such obvious aids are declared at enrolment. Prior to training commencement, the training provider and presenter should have adjusted access and egress as well as suitable seating within the training room and learning areas.

The best possible assistance to learning should be offered to all participants.

Chapter 5

Nonverbal Communication and Body Language

Nonverbal communication and body language is simply communicating without words. This included body positioning, leg and arm movements. Hand gestures and touching. It also includes micro expressions such as eye and mouth movement. These can give meaning and context to what is being said but also the hidden meaning of what is not being said. Important interpretations can be made by these 'paralanguages.' Stance and posture and even spatial distance can present important and possibly vital nonverbal messages.

> *'What is said is important however what is not being said is vital to understanding.'*
>
> – David W. Mayne

A trainer/assessor can win or lose individuals or a group of participants at initial contact by the nonverbal communication displayed. The body language of an educator combined with verbal projections can portray authority, knowledge, friendliness, assuredness and compassion. It can also portray nervousness, ignorance, anger, hostility and disinterest.

Body language can be presented by an individual consciously, unconsciously and innately. Our learned responses are formulated from birth and research has shown that even pre-natal influences and hereditary genetics may have contributing factors to the way an individual presents nonverbal communication when interacting with others. Over the years, an individual may change or adapt their body language and other nonverbal communication presentations through observation of others and assessing others' negative, positive or even quizzical responses to their own nonverbal presentations. It may also come from external chastisement or open verbal correction from others. An individual's ability to formulate, express and learn effective nonverbal communication is often dependent upon the individual's emotional intelligence and cognitive abilities relating to that individual's communicative processes, which are based on thought, reasoning, logic and interpretation.

Some elements that contribute to an individual's nonverbal communication development include:

- Genetics
- Parental and sibling interactions
- Education
- Peer base
- Trauma
- Geographic location
- Social demographics
- Cultural and religious influences
- Any prejudices (incoming or outgoing)

All these influences can have as much impact upon the development of nonverbal communication as it may on verbal communication.

Like a fingerprint or an iris scan, nonverbal communication presented by an individual is a unique attribute of that individual. From early life to death, an individual has innately and through learned behaviour including correction, develops their own individual body language that they present to others. This fingerprint of communication may change or vary either slightly, partially or significantly in certain situations that require variation to convey a message or give an adequate response. This adaptation is especially important in learning environments. Effective knowledge of how to present and use a trainer/educator's verbal and nonverbal communication skills can give a productive advantage in a learning environment. The use of nonverbal skills as an adult educator can portray to an individual or group of learners the meaning and importance of a word, sentence or topic being presented.

Stance and Body Frame

At the apex of a learning environment is the facilitator. The trainer/assessor is the focal point of delivery, therefore how that individual presents themselves physically may determine the participants' perceptions of the facilitator and the topic to be delivered.

Our frame of reference at stand to attention is the line of our shoulders down our arms, torso and legs to the outside of each foot (see diagram). While delivering a session our feet should be in alignment with our shoulders. This means that our feet are not together but slightly apart, directly beneath each shoulder point in an upright stance. This stance does not mean that the facilitator should remain rigid during the delivery of the whole session. It is to be considered a positional term of reference.

Arm and hand movement should be minimal and controlled. In most delivery situations it is advisable that a facilitator contain their hand and arm movements within their personal frame of reference. Avoid robotic, staccato movements as this can be distracting as well as possibly moving the aim of the presentation from the desired outcome.

Hand and arm movement in an educational environment can be a useful delivery tool for accentuating or emphasising points or as a means of smoothly flowing from one point to another. It can also quell disruptions or demonstrate a serious or deliberate point to participants to ponder. These movements only need to be small, subtle movements of the facilitator's arms, hands or fingers to emphasise, prioritise or diminish a point, or lead participants smoothly in the educational direction required by the facilitator to complete a specific element of training/education.

Positioning of feet and minimising leg movement is vital in presenting in an education environment. Feet should be spaced no further apart than the distance between the shoulders. This allows for smooth, subtle movements that don't distract from what the facilitator is trying to deliver to the participants.

Nervousness and unfamiliarity with the subject content may cause a facilitator to unconsciously move their legs and feet in an irregular, repetitious or erratic manner. This can present itself in the form of twitchy or tapping feet, or spontaneous knee movements when either standing or sitting. Moderation of this requires self-awareness by the facilitator to minimise physical manifestations of nerves or apprehension that may present themselves. It may require that the facilitator learns to modify their behaviour. This may be an instant cessation of this behaviour or require practice to stop this potentially disruptive, involuntary body movement.

Self-awareness is the key to resolving these issues and it is important that a facilitator observes participants and their possible reactions to any involuntary movements by the facilitator. This may be that participants are looking or staring at the distracting feet, legs or even arm and hand movements, or there may be flicking eye movement and general participant agitation. As a facilitator, check to see if this participant agitation is directly related to your own body movement and if it is, ensure that you consciously modify any distracting movements.

Eye Contact and Movement

Cicero (106-43 B.C.) is quoted as saying, '*Ut imago est animi voltus sic indices oculi.*' (*The face is a picture of the mind as the eyes are its interpreter*) (*Emotion Perception Across Cultures*, 2016).

The French say, '*Les yeux sont le miroir de l'âme.*' (*The eyes are the mirror of the soul*).

Over the centuries, proverbs have been written professing similar messages, that the eyes are the mirror to the soul and reflect everything that seems hidden. Like a mirror, they also reflect the person looking into them.

Eye contact and eye movement are crucial nonverbal communication tools and must never be taken lightly in a training/education environment. This is equally important for participants as it is for a trainer/facilitator. Communication can be greatly enhanced by combining clear verbal messages with matching eye movement and micro expressions.

Eyes react and present in many and varied ways depending upon several key stimuli such as:

- Physical Environment
- Setting
- Surrounding nonverbal communication
- Mood or state of being
- Physical wellness
- Individual personality/character
- Transference of meaning
- Verbal stimuli
- Response

Our eyes hide extraordinarily little from the true meaning or intent of what we want to communicate to another individual. Often words and eyes do not communicate in sync or parallel. What is being said can often be diametrically opposite to what the eyes are revealing.

If eye movement is flicking, side to side or up and down, this may mean that the facilitator/trainer or the learner is not confident in what they are saying or what is being said to them. For a facilitator, this could be because of a lack of knowledge or preparation of the topic being presented, or even trying to mislead or falsely convince participants about knowledge and understanding that the presenter doesn't have.

For the participant it may be due to a concern that the facilitator might call on them for input (spotlighting) or may be due to the participant not having the required knowledge or understanding.

To determine eye movement accurately, an observer must have a baseline of normal behaviour for reference. This goes for all nonverbal and verbal communication when it comes to intent determination. Over time and with significant interaction with an individual, familiarity with that individual's use of verbal and nonverbal presentations is attained and a baseline of normal behaviour is formed. Any variation to this usually means that an individual has been influenced by an external factor that triggers a variation from that baseline of normal verbal or nonverbal presentation. An individual's eyes are a major factor to observe when it comes to micro expressions.

Other facial expressions (micro expressions) can also tell a story about an individual that their words cannot.

The raising of an eyebrow may mean that that individual is questioning the validity of what another individual is telling them. Both eyebrows raised along with opening the eyes more than usual may mean that the individual is lying or not confident that what they are saying is accurate or trustworthy. A tilt of the head while speaking may mean that the individual is trying to portray sincerity, or if listening may doubt the sincerity of what's being said.

Tilting of the head up or down may have various meanings. Chin up with eyes looking up may mean that the individual is lying or searching their memory for information.

If eye contact is deliberate and forced (known as 'rods of steel'), that may mean that they don't want the observer to think they are lying by averting direct eye contact. However, this is usually presented as forced, manufactured and insincere.

Head and eyes down may be an indication that the individual is lying, guilty or unsure of the validity of the information they are trying to relay.

The pressing one's lips together may indicate that an individual has an opinion or information that they don't wish to disclose. Alternatively, they do want to disclose a thought or emotion without using negative words and would like their facial expression to convey the desired message. This may be a nonverbal manifestation of sarcasm. A fixed-lipped smile may also convey a message of disbelief or unhappiness. This is a prime example of how a feeling, thought or emotion can be presented with diametrically opposed micro expressions.

Nonverbal Punctuations

While full stops, commas, exclamation marks and many other grammatical symbols organise our written languages, face-to-face presentation uses appropriate verbal and nonverbal behaviour to apply the correct and necessary grammar to participants.

Nonverbal punctuations should align with verbally presented information or audio-visual presentations. If the nonverbal signals do not align or compliment what's being said in a presentation, participants may get contradicting, conflicting or misleading messages.

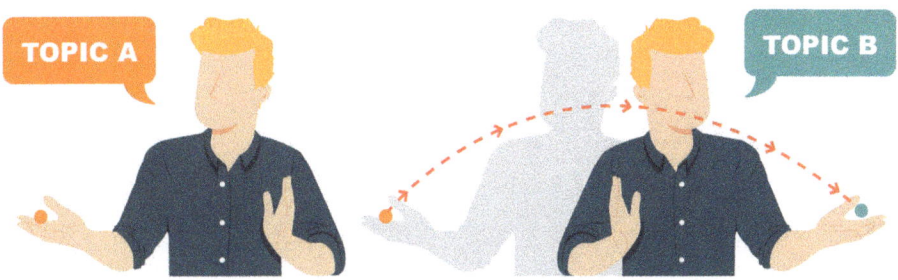

If the presenter/facilitator wishes to change from a section of delivery or one topic to another they can use smooth but deliberate transition moves with arms, hands and fingers still within their body's frame of reference. You can accentuate a change of topic or subject but subtly moving one hand away from the other and cease movement from the first hand and keep moving the hand and fingers of the other hand. This nonverbal movement along with verbal variations produces a smooth change in topic. You can also illicit a topic change by using a subtle slight turn or lean of the body in relation to your position within your range of delivery. This nonverbal variation is an excellent use of the contrast effect.

Chapter 6

Language Structure and Form

Linguistics

For any educator, facilitator, presenter or public who uses their voice and their language to convey meaning to others it is important and even fundamental to have a basic understanding of what language is, how it is used and more importantly how you can use it as a facilitator/presenter.

Not only does a knowledge of language, structure and form help you in presenting information to others, it may help you in greater understanding those who are presenting information to you.

This chapter only contains some basic definitions however, it is a starting point for your own inquiry into the structure and form of communication.

Linguistics – The study of Linguistics deals with language presentation and structure. This includes the many elements of language including grammar and phonetics.

Colloquial Language – Slang or colloquial language may vary greatly from nationality and cultural differences. Generally, slang is not formal language and is often concise abbreviations of more formal terminology.

Grammar – Grammar in both verbal and nonverbal communication relies on rules of structure both written and spoken. This includes such areas as syntax and morphology. With wider influences such as semantics and phonetics.

Syntax – Examines the processes and rules that put sentences together. This includes word placement that gives a sentence meaning.

Sociolinguistics – Is a discipline dealing with the influences that Language has in a community or even a culture. Individual social determination can dictate factors such as class or regional differences and even hierarchical ordering within a community.

Dialectology – Is the study of linguistics that examines dialects. It studies any even slight changes in language based on location or geographic distribution. This area of linguistics is related to sociolinguistics.

Semantics – Studies what language and words mean in linguistics. It examines how meaning in sentences can relate to each other or not at all.

Psycholinguistics – Studies the link between psychological and neurobiological factors and there link to linguistic behaviour.

Computational linguistics – Is linguistics from a computer or computational interpretation. The creation of speech and language is synthesised and presented by a computer.

Pragmatism – Is the practical use of words as a means to problem solve or even predict and rejects the idea that thought describes or reflects reality. Philosophically speaking a pragmatist observes that belief, science and meaning are best seen for their practical use.

Comparative Linguistics – The study of the differences and similarities between languages. These differences may manifest due to geographic or cultural reasons and even examining a languages slang variations.

Structural Linguistics – Sees language as a series of joining or interrelated structures. Structural Linguistics uses language and semiotics to clearly define elements of sentences.

Lexicon – A study of the way people speak. Their language, dialect and even accent. This may include slang and how that language expresses knowledge and understanding.

Morphology – The formation and study of words in language. It looks at word relationships in the same language. It also studies how words influence context in relation to stress and intonation.

Historical Linguistics – How over time language evolves and changes. Study current languages and analyse in reverse through history a languages roots, comparing developing linguistics over a period of time.

Chapter 7

Safety

As an educator/presenter that may work in many different venues and varying locations, it is important to know the health and safety requirements of:

- The organisation provider
- The venue being used
- The participants/audience
- Legislative requirements
- The course or topic being presented.

The reason a sound knowledge of workplace health and safety is important is that modern adult education bases itself on vocational or workplace practical examples, both within and outside the education facility. The wellbeing of all stakeholders is vitally important for the individuals, but also the organisation's reputation.

The RTO's presenters and participants all have organisational and individual obligations regarding health and safety. Adhering to and complying with legislated and organisational requirements may allow for minimal disruptions and higher completion of educational objectives.

Most workplaces require specific legal knowledge, skills and practice requirements.

These can be broken down into two areas:

1. Health and Safety requirements
2. Specific Workplace Requirements

Health and Safety

Although most organisations have their own internal workplace health and safety protocols and regulations, government agencies and related departments have mandatory health and safety regulations for all workplaces that are legislative by construct, design and implementation. A breach of these legislations may incur warnings, breach notices or steep fines to both employee and employer. Severe penalties to an organisation may include the shutting down of a workplace, potentially terminating the employment of all employees.

All workplaces should have a schedule of regular on-going health and safety training factored into their strategic and operational plans, as well as into their annual budgets. The content of this training may vary dependent upon changes in workplace operation or legislative changes relating to industry specific health and safety. It must be a priority in all workplaces that appropriate and specific workplace training is undertaken at the instigation of that workplace's management or health and safety officer.

In an attempt to reduce workplace accidents and personnel downtime in Australia, each State and Territory has introduced Occupational (Workplace) Health and Safety (WHS) legislation. Its purpose is to increase awareness of work safety standards, protocols and requirements and empower employers and employees on issues relating to health and safety in the workplace.

Because employees are responsible for maintaining a safe workplace for self, others and property, a workplace's managers, supervisors and team leaders will need to ensure that appropriate information is available for all employees to easily access.

Generally, staff will refer to their organisation's internal health and safety policies and procedures. However, WHS information is available from within an organisation and from external resources, such as government agencies.

Within an organisation, information sources include:

- Work Health and Safety Guidelines and Manual
- Organisation's Policy and Procedure Manual
- Organisation reports
- Incident reports
- Staff memos
- Other staff members including other team leaders, WHS representatives and human resources staff

You can also find WHS information in:

- State legislation
- Workplace cover
- Professional journals and organisations
- Books
- Newspapers articles
- Trade unions

State or Regional Legislation

Each state produces its own health and safety legislation made up of 'Acts' and 'Codes of Practice' for the purpose of improving health and safety within the workplace.

The Acts provide a framework which allows employers and employees flexibility to achieve the required standards which are set out in the Acts. The Acts aim to:

- Ensure the health, safety and welfare of all people at work
- Protect other members of the public and contractors at the workplace

- Promote a working environment which meets the physical and psychological needs of employees
- Provide a framework based on the Codes of Practice

The Acts cover:

- The employer's duty of care (or responsibilities)
- The employee's duty of care
- How the Act is enforced

The aim of the Codes of Practice is to give a practical guide and detail issues that are covered in the Acts. These are revised from time to time to keep pace with changes and developments in the workplace and the law. It is vital that regular reviews of policy and the related Acts occur to keep up to date with any new changes.

Specific Workplace Requirements

This refers to workplace requirements specific to the individual undertaking their regular workplace duties that relate directly to their job description and broader scope of employment and staff development.

Workplaces can be similar, especially those within the same or aligning industries, but there will always be many differences that may include operational protocols and systems, management styles, and related ancillary services or partners. Organisations may also operate under the legislation of different government bodies for each state, territory, region, country or even local government authority. There may be small but very specific variations to the legislative requirements for identical organisations or franchises operating within different government bodies.

It is important that all staff are made aware of those workplace variances. This can be achieved through vocational training, ensuring that they gain the required skills and knowledge to efficiently and effectively undertake their duties.

Macro and Micro Workplace Vocational Learning

Macro workplace vocational learning relates to legislation, localised rules and codes of practice. This includes all workplace legislations in place from any tier of government or government gazetted departments, as well as organisational rules, protocols and codes of practice that are specific to that workplace. Industry regulations are also covered under Macro education requirements. This generally refers to specific industry related codes of practice.

Micro workplace vocational learning are those workplace elements that may be hard to qualify and can include personality, character or behaviour traits of peer workers, management and ancillary staff.

An example of Micro learning would be this advice to a new employee: 'Don't ask John for anything in the morning until he has had his first cup of coffee.' This refers directly to John the co-worker and his inability to communicate in an effective and courteous manner prior to the day's initial caffeine intake.

Sometimes it is necessary within an organisation to understand the behaviour and idiosyncrasies of co-workers in order to facilitate a harmonious and productive working environment. This does not mean that you enter into adverse banter or accept negative, destructive or unproductive behaviour within a workplace, but rather become aware of best operational management at a micro level. Having said that, negative, destructive or unproductive workplace behaviour must be reported if it has or may cause damage to self, others or property, or if it impinges negatively on the day-to-day duties of any staff member when undertaking their roles.

Chapter 8

Workplace Education for Professional or Personal Growth

Existing Workers

An individual may feel that to progress or become better established in their workplace, it is necessary to be further educated/qualified. Some organisations offer internal training to staff in courses relevant to the roles and responsibilities of that specific employee. If the sought-after education is outside the job scope of the employee, they may need to seek external training at a vocational education training facility that delivers the desired course.

It is not uncommon for some organisations to offer staff development courses to employees as an avenue of personal and professional growth for their staff. Common workplace education may include courses in:

- Health and safety (usually mandatory)
- Customer service
- Interpersonal skills
- Dealing with difficult people
- Working in a team environment and team building
- Cultural awareness
- Communication

- Leadership and Management
- Personal time management

There are many other staff development courses that an employer may offer an employee, including course subjects that relate directly to an area of individual or organisational operation. This training is for the benefit of the employee and may be factored into the organisation's strategic and operational plan as well as budgeted for in annual financial planning. Courses may be undertaken internally through appropriately qualified and accredited trainers or outsourced to contracted trainers or external vocational institutions.

An individual staff member may take it upon themselves to undertake training as a means of attaining personal growth or as an avenue for employment elsewhere. Further education may also be a means of intellectual expansion or stimulation, or simply a way of avoiding workplace boredom.

A job service provider or government employment service may encourage or insist that a client undertake certain training. The job service provider can then improve the structure and content of their client's resume, helping to improve that client's prospects of future employment.

Corrective services institutions run courses for inmates to better their chances for employment once released, as well as helping the processes of rehabilitation and minimising the chances of reoffending by keeping inmates occupied, especially those with extensive term convictions and embedded mind sets.

Volunteer or not-for-profit community-based organisations may also feel it would benefit their volunteers if specific training was given as a way of organisational and personal growth. Volunteer organisations operate more efficiently if their staff are better equipped in knowledge and skills.

Individuals that are well-established in their particular vocation may feel dissatisfied in their chosen careers or may have a desire to change professions and interests. To accomplish this, they need to acquire education or qualifications to aid in that desired new profession.

A great number of organisations instigate internal staff development programs for employees. These education programs are often included in operational budgets and internal or external trainers commissioned to undertake this staff development. Organisations utilising these internal programs show good governance and sound business acumen.

Staff are encouraged to attend, though in most professional situations it is mandatory for staff to attend. This allows them to gain new skills, knowledge and insights that will not only help them in their current workplace but also allow staff the opportunity for professional and fiscal advancement.

Work Experience

Many learning institutions such as schools, secondary education bodies and universities have programs in place for vocational experience. This is where individuals are given opportunities to nominate a profession of interest to the educational body, which will then make an arrangement with an accessible organisation in the desired vocation/industry. A placement then occurs over a set period of time where the participant can learn on site through discussion, observation and question and answer sessions with management and/or employees about the organisation and industry. This knowledge can be obtained through site tours or in the organisation's specifically allocated training room. These areas of training should abide by general education presentation requirements such as suitable size, air flow, lighting and relevant audio-visual technology as well as demonstration material such as typical resources used in that industry.

From the industry host's perspective, it is imperative that the organisation's presenters are equipped with proficient knowledge of not only the organisation and its industry, but also the knowledge and skills to train and impart onto others regarding the industry.

To attain a pathway for better training, the host organisation should, at the completion of the work experience program, present a survey/feedback form to be completed by the participant and a separate form for the participant's learning institution. Information from both forms is valuable to the organisation to ascertain appropriateness, content and effectiveness of the workplace experience for the participants, allowing for host improvement. The learning institution should also survey and gain feedback from the participant and the host organisation to gain information about the organisation, changes in the related industry and the participant's perception of their own experience. This could confirm that the participant's interest in the industry should be developed or not.

Chapter 9

Presentation and Presentation

One of the most important factors in presenting information to individuals or groups is how we personally present ourselves to others. Another is how that information is presented to those same people.

There are several key factors that determine how a trainer, lecturer or facilitator should present themselves and their information to the participants present. The determining factors are as follows:

- Who are the participants?
- What are you teaching?
- Where are you teaching?
- What is the time frame of delivery?
- Who is the training provider?
- Is it internal or external training?

Who Are They?

Knowledge of the participants is fundamental. You need to know who they are and what organisation/industry they come from. Why are they there? Are they there for staff development training? Personal growth or interest? Are they following a mandatory directive? It is unnecessary for the participant to divulge if they are there through a discipline procedure, but they may offer this confidential information to you during the training.

Are the participants from a disadvantaged or privileged socio-economic background? This makes no difference on *what* is delivered but may significantly determine *how* you deliver a session. The core outcomes of the session must not be changed, but you can consider a variation to delivery method without detracting from the key learning elements.

What and Where are you Training?

Your physical appearance in front of a class is determined just as much by what is being delivered as where it is being delivered. It would be ludicrous for a trainer to turn up in a farm paddock delivering a session on changing diesel oil in a 75-horsepower tractor dressed in a three-piece suit. It would also be just as inappropriate for a trainer to deliver a session on strategic plan design and implementation for senior managers dressed in overalls and sandals.

The golden rule is comfortable, suitable and, above all, professional. For example, if your environment is hot, dry and sunny, then wear clothes that suit that environment while simultaneously reflecting you, your organisation, your students and the topic to be delivered.

I made a big mistake many years ago when delivering a session within a correctional facility to a group of inmates referred to as 'long termers'. The work was hot and hard outdoor work. The inmates wore prison-issue greens. Either a short sleeve denim shirt or cotton singlet and shorts. I was overheating in my open neck shirt and dress slacks. After a long day I vowed to return for the next session in much more comfortable and suitable attire. Was I wrong?

I arrived in the normal clothing I would wear for delivering the session, however underneath I wore a blue singlet and blue shorts. About an hour into the session, I discarded my outer clothing and proceeded to continue with the session under the relentless sun. The inmates working with me were nonplussed about my new look until a senior corrective officer drew me aside and professionally but adamantly admonished me for my unprofessional attire. He requested that I change immediately, or I would be escorted from the facility. My only thoughtless response was, 'I made sure they were blue not green,' at which the senior guard just looked me in the eye, withholding his retort. I hastily changed into my original clothing.

I have also delivered many high-level business management courses over many years and ensure that I wear a suit or at least a collar and tie. Depending on the topic and the participants, it is a good learning strategy to adjust that formal clothing state a little as a tool of delivery. In a business management session, an air of determination and 'getting down to business' can be achieved by removing the coat, rolling up the sleeves and unbuttoning the top collar. It is important to carefully place the jacket over a chair or hang nearby to give the participants a sense of still being professional and caring about my appearance. This delivery strategy should only be used when the trainer is at the stage of the topic or session where such a move would not only give credence and validity to the subject but gain respect for the trainer. A trainer should also be aware of any particular dress code by the training organisation for its trainers as well the dress code wherever the training is being undertaken.

Remember these three things when deciding what to wear: comfortable, suitable and above all professional, as you are not only representing yourself and your training institution employer, but also the industry-based topic you're delivering. In doing this, you prepare the participant for what they may come to expect of workplace personal presentation.

How do I Present to Others?

Knowledge, experience and skill mean very little if we can't efficiently and effectively transfer those skills and knowledge to others in a vocational education environment.

Confidence is derived from acquiring, retaining and being able to transfer knowledge to others, as well as your personal standing as a public speaker. When you present yourself in front of a participant or group of participants, it's always good to be a little nervous. It means that your adrenalin is up, as you care about the participants and the topic that you want to deliver. The issue is if your nerves and awkwardness is related to the fact that you are not confident or familiar with the material of the session. If you are not confident in your knowledge of the subject matter to be presented, then the discerning participants will perceive that uneasiness very quickly and they too may not have confidence in what is being presented to them. It comes back to one of the three foundation pillars of education: Know your **Topic**, Know your **Audience** and Know your **Venue (TAV)**.

If you are comfortable that you have the knowledge and experience that you can pass on to others, then you are well on your way towards settling your nerves and presenting with confidence and authority. This can come through revising the material, undertaking one's own relevant training, or practical observation.

As a former worker and trainer in the radio industry, it was important to train not only new announcers and other on-air personnel, but also to train the trainer so others were able to transfer knowledge and skills acquired to new employees.

Rod was a 47-year-old man who had been a radio presenter for over twenty years. He had been both a news reader and a program presenter, but also dabbled in promotions and public relations with various radio stations at different times. Rod expressed a huge amount of self-assurance. The type of person who commanded a room full of people when he walked into it. His presented persona was an innate air of confidence and authority.

During his mandatory 'train the trainer' sessions, Rod maintained this confidence and assurance. His knowledge and experience base were never questioned. However, I was concerned at his seemingly overconfident attitude to training, as he continually professed his ability to 'hold a class in the palm of his hand'. Rod maintained that his lesson plans and course notes were all in his head. I told him of my concerns regarding session preparation and course notes. Then Rod told me that it was all in hand and that I should not be worried. This concerned me even more as I hold enormous credence with lesson preparation and session delivery notes.

The time came when Rod was to present to a room full of new staff members on practical application of on-air presentation. Rod walked into the room beaming with the confidence I was accustomed to. There were only six participants planted in a line of chairs directly in front of the desk where Rod was to present from. Rod gave a brief introduction of himself as rehearsed, then conducted a short icebreaker activity.

The actual course session was about to begin when Rod changed tack and proceeded to talk more about himself, going back to his history as a youth listening to radio. Yes, Rod made it interesting, but it was irrelevant and unnecessary to the structure, content and delivery of this course. The participants listened politely, glancing at their watches. As a session observer, I was unable to intervene and sat quietly taking some notes as discussed with Rod prior to his session.

Rod continued to discuss himself and his career until at last a participant politely interjected with, 'I'm sorry but the lesson is nearly half over, and we haven't started yet.' At this point Rod looked a little hurt and disgruntled and retorted, 'This is part of the lesson' and paused to look at the non-existent notes on his desk. The lesson, not to mention the facilitator's credibility, was lost and it would take something special to win the class back. This wasn't the worst part of Rod's introduction to face-to-face training.

Rod began to speak on the topic we agreed based on all those years of knowledge and experience. He was lost. What was presented was a disjointed and irrelevant barrage of obscure facts with no set direction or progression. The participants gave up writing notes, stared blankly ahead, perplexed and confused.

At the end of the session, Rod walked past me at the back of the room and quietly stated 'Well, that went very well.' At our review session a little later, I explained why it hadn't.

As stated earlier, Rod had all the knowledge, skill and experience but was unable to transfer those elements to a small group of eager people. Some might say that ego overshadowed ability in this case. A little bit of planning wouldn't have gone astray either.

Although Rod never had that particular class again, he did learn some valuable teaching skills. In future sessions he was able to hold the attention of a group and transfer that wealth of experience to them, helping to produce some wonderful on-air presenters for the radio industry.

Time Frame of Delivery

In your preparation and delivery, always consider the topic, the desired outcomes and how the topic fits into the overall plan and design of the subject or course.

Questions to be asked include:

- What is the course?
- What is the topic?
- What do you hope to deliver in a session?
- How long is the session?
- Is there a practical component?
- Is there in session assessment required?
- How many participants will or should be present?
- Is this a follow-on session from a previous related session?
- Is this session a prerequisite for the next future session?

When you have determined adequate answers to these questions, then the planning and execution of this session should be much easier when considering a probable limited time frame of delivery.

In preparation for a session, determine the crucial elements that you wish to cover. Ensure that you give yourself enough time to address all elements and outcomes that are course requirements but are also comfortably able to be delivered within the timeframe of the allocated session. Avoid trying to fit too much into a session, as this may mean rushing topics that could disadvantage the participants. If you drag a session out, participants may feel discouraged or bored with not only the session, but potentially the topic and the course.

Allocate elements of the session in line with required outcomes. Larger or more important elements, or those with significant outcomes, may require a larger portion of the session plan. Think of it as a pie graph. If you divide the session into pie pieces then those elements of great importance should have a larger piece of the time pie.

You can colour-coordinate your chart. For example, red may indicate a crucial or poignant element of the session whereas green may be still significant but less crucial.

Note: this visual allocation of priority is for the facilitator's use in session preparation and should not be presented to the participants.

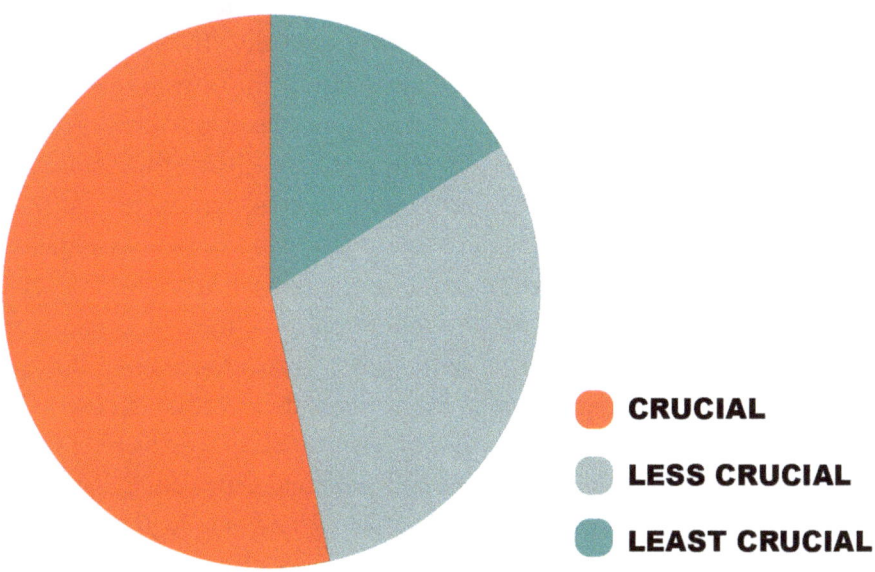

Who is the Training Provider?

Which course is delivered is determined by the training provider. It is the governing body that determines what courses are within the registered training organisation's scope. These providers may be government or private sector organisations. Some providers may only specialise in certain vocational areas and therefore only have a small number of related and specific courses on their scope for delivery. Other providers may have a large number of courses on their scope and cater for various industry and scholastic areas.

These are the organisational bodies that employ you and therefore pay you. They may determine a great deal of your organisation requirements, including policy and protocols. They must adhere to government-determined course requirements and be compliant as a service provider in fulfilling these requirements, including delivery and assessment outcomes. In summary, a higher organisational body determines if a training provider has complied with all delivery and assessment requirements. This means that the training provider's facilitators must also provide evidence that these elements have been completed.

Is it Internal or External Training?

The training provider and the facilitator must determine if the course/session will be delivered internally or externally. Internal training means that the participants attend sessions within a training facility provided by the training provider, usually a classroom or simulated workplace environment. External training will be outside the classroom. Resources provided by the training provider and can either be in a specific workplace area that is onsite or at a specific workplace separate to the training provider. External training may have an industry focus. For example, the theoretical component of a course on broad acre crop raising may be done internally within a classroom environment supplied by the training provider. However, some practical and specific industry related elements of broad acre farming may be delivered on site on a broad acre farm giving direct and practical experience. Farmside delivery and relevant assessments may be carried out in this external environment.

Chapter 10

Suitable Suits

A trainer/facilitator's appearance and personal presentation may determine how that individual is received by participants, which can in turn influence how those participants receive, process and retain information given by that facilitator. Initial personal presentation and appearance can often determine the level of respect that participants have for their facilitator and determine if that particular education scenario will be successful or not.

In colloquial terms, it is a 'horses for courses' approach. There are many variants that decide the best way a trainer/facilitator should physically present themselves in the way they dress. These variants should be considered before you step out your door on day one of your delivery session.

Who is the organisation providing the education? What is their dress code, if any?

The way we dress to deliver a session for an organisation may be influenced by the scope of that particular organisation. Any fundamental or guiding ideologies may influence dress code to the point of even being required to wear an organisational uniform with corporate insignia attached. This may happen with large multinational organisation with international branding or religious based organisations that have well-defined protocols regarding dress.

This brings uniformity to all trainers and other staff. It does at times attempt to remove individualism from trainers in the hope of not singling out any particular educator as better or worse than another. This attempt at uniformity aims to establish a neutrality within an organisation as well as using the uniform and attached branding as a marketing/promotional tool.

Other organisations may have strict or somewhat strict dress codes that reflect the professionalism that that particular organisation wishes to present.

An example of organisational dress requirements is within corrective services organisations (prisons). It is required for trainers to be discreet with how they dress, not emphasising their gender or sexuality. There are reasons for this in a corrective service organisation not needed to be expanded upon in this book. In this particular environment a trainer/facilitator should dress and present themselves professionally and discreetly.

Because of the potential for many and varied training environments within a correction facility, temperature and other environmental factors may determine suitable variations to clothing to be worn. In such a facility, it may be required to wear a personal security alarm such as a 'duress' button. This is normally attached to a belt. At other times you may be mandatorily required to wear a two-way radio unit with pre-set frequency allocation.

The dress needs of a correctional facility may vary from centre to centre. It is important therefore that you gain as much information regarding clothing to be worn from each individual correctional facility. Do not assume that all correctional facilities have the same uniform dress codes.

Another question to consider is who are the participants/clients? Understand the demographic of the participants. Note individual paradigms and how they might fit with others in the group. What is the program, course, session you are delivering? What is the content or theme of your delivery session? The content will often determine your dress and personal presentation.

Once you have been engaged by an education provider, it is important that you gain knowledge of a broad profile of the participants you will be presenting to. Are they a selection of randomly enrolled people or are they from a particular organisation or industry? Are they unemployed or perhaps have physical disability or mental health issues? None of these factors change the way the content is delivered. However, it may influence in certain circumstances how a facilitator dresses as a potential delivery tool.

For example, if the course is a practical onsite horticulture course and the session is planting skills and irrigation, it is not a practical or appropriate to dress in business attire. This does not mean that the facilitator should dress unprofessionally, but they should wear attire that suits the profession. The facilitator is still representing not only the training organisation or the industry associated with the session, but also themselves. A professional impression may be the difference between engaging participants or giving participants a false impression of the facilitator's ability to be able impart knowledge with authority. Neat, tidy and appropriate dress is an easy formula to follow, as well as thoughtful consideration of the participants socio-economic circumstances.

Where are you physically delivering can be a huge factor in determining what you can and should wear when delivering a session.

Environmental factors contribute greatly to how a trainer/facilitator should dress. These include climate and weather as well as whether the session will be delivered within or outside a room, building or enclosure. The formula of neat, tidy and appropriate still holds credence in any environment with the added variable of suitability. It would not be practical or comfortable to dress unsuitably for harsh weather conditions such as wind, cold, heat or rain. However, organisational dress code requirements, if applicable, must be adhered to. Training providers' dress guidelines will allow for conditions relating to changing weather conditions or delivery location. It is advisable to wear clothes that are not brand names or seen as trendy or elitist. A facilitator wearing these garments may make some participants feel uneasy or even slightly degraded. Once again, knowledge of the participants is a respectful consideration by a trainer, and an expression of that knowledge by wearing appropriate attire to a session will help enforce respect.

Strategic Dressing

Can a trainer/facilitator make impact or strategic point with how they dress for a delivery session?

A facilitator can have a huge impact on participants by gaining respect and engagement through the way they dress and visually present themselves.

If the training is in business management or leadership then it's prudent for the trainer to dress with industry appropriateness. If that appropriateness means wearing a suit and tie, then you as the facilitator should set an industry example and dress accordingly.

Chapter 11

Room Set-up and Configurations

Let's boldly assume that you know the subject you're going to present and that you know where your participants are from. You must also have knowledge of where the training will take place and at what time your delivery session commences. You should have knowledge of the class set-up, including the participants desk/chair positioning, as well as your delivery station in relation to participants, whiteboard, supporting resources such as demonstration and audio-visual equipment, and display screens.

To position your desk, lectern or chair at the front and middle of the room may be a visual distraction or impediment for the participant's view of the board or AV displays. This will depend on what's being presented. If you and your words are predominately the focus of that particular session's delivery, then a central and front location is practical and efficient.

If there is a high ratio of whiteboard, smart board or AV presentation needed for the session, then the facilitator's station should be at the front and to the side of the room, away from the wall and entrances. This allows for excellent participant views to you and any front-of-room displays, as well as better opportunity for interaction with participants.

There are several participant desk configurations that may include 'theatre style', where all tables and chairs are placed in consecutive rows facing the front of the class. 'Boardroom style' is generally for smaller groups where participants sit around a large rectangular table with the trainer assuming the head or chair of that configuration. Any boards or displays are presented behind or slightly to the side of the trainer. 'Islands' of tables are placed around the room with up to eight participants at each table. This configuration allows for the trainer to move in-between the tables, interacting with students more freely. This configuration is more suited to workshop scenarios when more interaction with each other and the trainer is needed.

In most educational delivery environments, the best configuration within four walls and allowing for a single trainer/educator delivery is a 'U-shaped' set-up. This allows for mutual unrestricted visibility by participants and the person delivering the session. It also allows for easy access to the individual participant, if observing the participants' work is required or for the dispersal of resources from the educator. This configuration also gives unrestricted vision of any projected or written presentations at the front of the room.

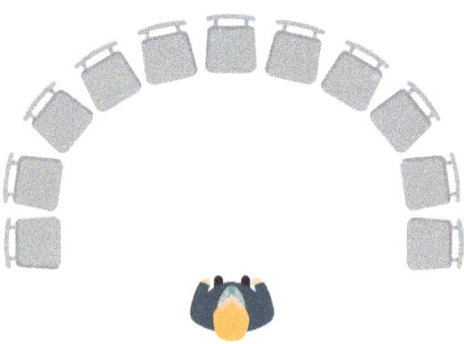

CHAPTER 11 ~ ROOM SET-UP AND CONFIGURATIONS

Auditoriums or larger venues may have fixed unmovable presenter stations. This isn't an issue regarding audio visual access by the participants, as display screens are more often than not placed high and to the back of where the presenter is situated. For even larger venues there may be several screens positioned throughout the space that participants situated anywhere are able to clearly view. Auditoriums and conference rooms are usually one level with perhaps a stage to elevate the presenter. Amphitheatres are similar in presentation requirements however the ascending rows of participants helps with interaction, observance and acoustics. Both these venues may require sound magnification through a microphone and speakers. Due to the engineering structure of the amphitheatre, microphone support may be less of an issue than a large auditorium or conference hall. The design and efficiencies of an amphitheatre goes back thousands of years and it is remarkable how effectively and acoustically designed these theatres are.

When presenting in an outdoor environment there are critical factors to consider. Conflicting noise is the major one, as interfering sound such as machinery or traffic can seriously impede the session by being a distraction for the participants and the facilitator. The message to be delivered can be greatly distorted or even missed all together by external noises. This is frustrating for both trainer and student. A factory setting, or other areas of machinery use can have similar interference.

If the session is to be delivered in a noisy area, then the trainer must consider that this noise-filled environment is for demonstration purposes only, with theoretical components delivered elsewhere. In their session plan, the trainer should identify a 'sanctuary' area, free from interfering noise or activity. This is where the trainer can deliver the theoretical component of the session and prepare the participant for the demonstration that will have external noise.

Chapter 12

Lighting and Acoustics (The Sweet Spot)

Lighting and Sound

In any location the presenter is delivering a session, they must consider lighting and sound. In most cases, inadequate sound or lighting severely impedes the delivery and learning experience. The facilitator must have foreknowledge of both these vitally important elements at any venue that a session is to be delivered at.

See What Needs to be Seen

Never have lighting, including bright sunlit windows, behind the presenter. This creates a silhouette effect for the participants, who may only see a featureless shadow speaking to them. Participants want to be able to see who is talking to them and in effective communication, micro expressions are vital in the accurate transfer of information.

In an ideal training environment, lighting should be multifaceted. Lighting above the participants and the trainer should be bright and sharp while a light facing the trainer should be softer and warmer. This particular light may come from a roof-mounted spotlight. This is common in amphitheatres and auditorium scenarios but less common in a classroom setting.

The use of these lights will vary somewhat depending upon what is being delivered and where that delivery is being made. If the facilitator is delivering a session that requires only them and their AV to be observed, then the need for participant lighting can be lessened. This gives a theatre effect where only the presentation area is illuminated. If the learning environment requires that the participants take notes or interact with each other, then the lighting should be bright and sharp. For training rooms, the ideal light intensity is 500 lux with a colour rendering of 80Ra. This is only a recommendation as varying venues will allow for different lighting conditions. Factors to consider include shape of the room, the location of the facilitator and participants within the room, any external lighting such as windows and any energy conservation practices.

There are several important considerations for lighting design in training environments.

Every training organisation has a place, or several places, where they hold training, meetings and other gatherings. But what many organisations don't realise is how important the layout of a space and its lighting design are to what's being presented. In particular, the lighting of the room or other venue, can either facilitate productivity or hinder it. How is the optimal lighting determined?

- **Room Size**: How many people does the training space accommodate? Is it a small conference room or a large lecture hall? The size of the room is one of the most important considerations for lighting design in training spaces.

- **Energy Conservation**: The more lights you have in the space, the more energy you'll use. Think about ways to light the room without wasting energy. Large windows and skylights can help, but sunlight also fluctuates throughout the day, giving you less control over the light levels in the space. Consider using LED bulbs or other energy-saving methods.

- **Use of Technology**: Will a projection screen be in use in this room? Will participants be using their laptops, tablets, note pads or other devices? It's important that the lighting in the space not reflect off devices or overwhelm the projection screen and other AV tools, making the content difficult to see. Test your light levels based on what you plan on using the room for and the technology it will need to accommodate.

- **Appropriate Brightness**: If light levels are too low, it can make people drowsy during the session. On the other hand, if the lights are too bright, it's distracting, making people restless. Also consider appropriate light levels for taking notes and reading handouts or other materials. Also consider that some participants may have a level of vision impairment. Do some testing of your light levels to make sure you have the ideal brightness for the room.

- **Lighting Control**: There are many ways of controlling a room's lighting levels. You can have a series of switches, each controlling a small section of lights, allowing you to turn on just enough to get the level you need. You can have a dimmer switch that lets you adjust the levels of all the lights at once. For a large enough space, you can even have a lighting board that adjusts different sections individually to give you the perfect level for your purposes. If the feature of a session is an audio visual display then the room can be dimmed allowing the screen and display to stand out and for the participants to view in comfort. Take the time before a session to familiarise yourself with these controls.

How dark does the space get without light? How easy is it to find the lighting controls in the dark? Going through the space in the dark can lead to accidents. Many organisations make sure no one can enter an entirely dark room. They'll have motion sensors that turn on the lights just before someone enters, or pilot lights that are always on, providing just enough light to navigate and find a switch. Alternately, light switches are placed outside the door, so participants can turn it on manually as they go in.

There are a number of other important considerations for lighting design in meeting spaces. The right lighting design can increase a room's productivity and versatility. Think about what you need to do in the space, and research different lighting types that will accommodate those needs.

Now the whole group of eager participants can see you; however, that counts for very little if they can't hear what you need to present.

What You Say and How You Say It

Here are some factors to consider when thinking about sound: the venue's size and your relative position within it, the number of participants, and the architectural design of the classroom. These factors can dictate whether you need to use electronically amplified sound through a microphone and/or audio-visual sound support. Do not attempt to use your unassisted voice in an environment that does not carry sound well. You will fail miserably.

In a smaller room where voice carry is not as critical, it is important to grasp several basic but fundamental principles.

Positioning at the front of the room is vital. If you need to walk slightly in front of a board or display screen during a session, never have your back towards the screen. Always ensure that the front of your left shoulder never comes to the right of the furthest participant on left and never let you right shoulder come to the left of the furthest participant on your right.

A simple rule to go by is that if you are in the centre of the room at the front then you are at the 'apex' of your range of presentation. Facing the class from this spot, point to the furthest participant on your left with your left hand and point to the furthest participant to the right with your right hand. This is your range of delivery. Of course, this rule can be broken when you need to write something on the board. At those times, never address the class as only the board will hear you. If you need to directly address something on the board or display screen, then resume your front facing positioning but assume that the item you are drawing attention too is now at the apex of presentation. Position yourself either side of that apex point depending on whether you are right or left handed for pointing purposes (if required).

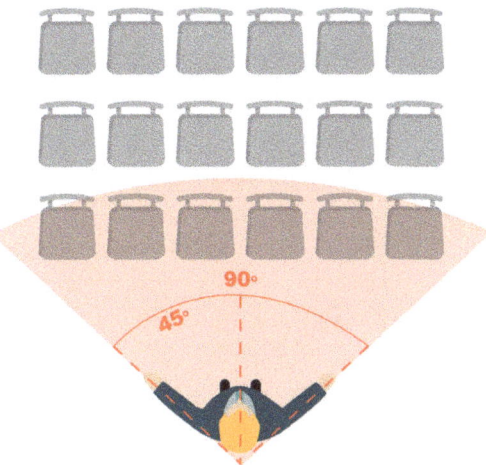

Body positioning and posture in front of a class can either capture the attention of a participant or distract them for the rest of the session. In their exuberance or displays of nervousness, some trainers choose to wave their arms around like a sports umpire or referee. This is unnecessary and distracting. Hand and arm movement can be an excellent tool for the trainer if used properly. Hand movements can assist in changing topics, emphasising points and help accurately punctuate what's being said. These movements must be natural and not over-rehearsed, or the result will be false, contrived, robotic and insincere, and participants may lack confidence in what the trainer is trying to relay. Some may question the authority of the trainer to deliver a specific topic. Small, slow hand movement within your torso frame are best, with occasional sorties outside that frame when wishing to change topics, emphasise a point or allude to an item on the board or display screen.

If you stand facing the participants, have your feet slightly apart so that they are situated directly under each shoulder. The vertical rectangle you form is your torso frame and this is a safe area to limit the range of your hand movements. Once you gain confidence of your own training capabilities and get to know your participants, then you will find it much easier and much more natural to step out of that safe frame and be able to freely express yourself.

If you are using a lectern or presenting from behind a desk, then incorporate the height and width of the lectern into your personal frame of delivery (PFD). The lectern is not a hiding place and is not to be used as a sanctuary for the nervous trainer. It is a tool to be used. Lecterns are not to be leant on or used as a side prop for a tired trainer. Lecterns or lecture desks often have microphones attached to them, so any movement that the presenter makes transfers straight to the house speakers and then to annoyed and distracted participants. Nervously tapping a pen or a finger on a lectern or desk with a microphone attached must not happen.

Minor tapping is amplified many times via the microphone. Hands placed either side of a lectern is satisfactory as long as it doesn't stifle your hand movements. The lectern is somewhere to place your notes and reference material for easy access and to help your voice carry if it supports a microphone. A lectern can also store AV controls and laser pointers when not being used. Stand up straight behind the lectern and resist the temptation to lean on or slouch behind it. Although this body language may demonstrate a sense of confidence and authority to some participants, it may also portray an air of arrogance and unprofessionalism. Overcompensation for a bad case of nerves or stage fright can also induce a trainer to slouch, with or without a lectern.

Chapter 13

Public Speaking Terrors and Voice Projection

'For some people pain of death is preferable to speaking in public.'

David W. Mayne

One of the greatest fears in life for some people is not spiders, snakes or sharks, but of being asked to stand in front of a group of people and speak. I have seen grown men and women so overcome with fear that they have been physically sick. One case passed out. There are those people who present a persona of enormous confidence and assuredness, yet the thought of speaking publicly can reduce them to a quivering mass of nerves and gibberish.

There are some simple tricks that can help overcome chronic nervousness before, during and after any public presentation. These are able to be put in practice by anyone and they coincide with some fundamental public speaking rules and practices.

What Not to Do

Do not drink alcohol, milk or orange juice before a speaking engagement. Alcohol is the big 'no no' for several reasons. Firstly, alcohol is a dehydrating agent that will directly affect your throat and voice box, distorting your speech and octave range. Secondly the physical and cognitive reactions to alcohol may severely impede your presentation through slurred or disjointed speech. Even a small amount of alcohol can change crucial public speaking elements such as pace, tone and volume. The sometimes relaxing and confidence-building side effects that alcohol brings may also be obvious in a negative way to an audience. Alcohol can transform a smooth and well-constructed presentation into an ill-constructed set of jumbled facts and intelligible rhetoric, entirely unbeknownst to the presenter. Others who have alcohol prior to public speaking seem to fall into a depressive state of low activity and closed body language. Their presentation will also have variations in tone, volume and pace, but monotone inflection may dominate what they are trying to say. Alcohol can transform speakers into a person they are not and that they eventually don't even recognise.

At one public speaking competition I was facilitating, I noticed one of the candidates was eating a meal with what seemed copious amounts of red wine prior to their presentation that one of the candidates was eating a meal with what seemed copious amounts of red wine. When he reached the lectern to deliver his talk, he slouched over the lectern, commenced his talk with an inappropriate comment then belittled the audience and judges for not laughing. He then had to leave the lectern to retrieve his forgotten notes that were at the back of the room. He presented his talk in a manner that made no sense. Although he was well-versed in the topic, he constantly strayed from it and continually interjected with irrelevant comments. After a while the audience began to laugh at just about everything he said. At the end he got stifled applause.

I spoke with him after the competition, in which he came in last place. He couldn't understand what he did wrong. In his alcohol-riddled mind he thought he did an excellent presentation and even commented on the fact that he had the audience completely engaged, as they were laughing at what he was saying. I agreed with him but added that they were actually laughing at him and how he was saying things. One judge's comments said, 'a comedy of sad errors', while another simply said, 'some people just shouldn't drink before they speak.' This candidate learned a valuable lesson that even if a person feels alcohol doesn't affect their public speaking, it usually does in an adverse way. The main issue is that most people don't even realise that they are being affected and the alcohol subtly blocks their ability to see what and how they are presenting.

Milk, other dairy products and orange juice can produce phlegm or mucous in the throat and mouth, as do a lot of other beverages and foods. This can be an individualised reaction. Be your own laboratory subject and test yourself on certain foods or drinks to see if they produce any adverse reactions that may impede your ability to speak. If you do get a reaction, then be mindful of avoiding that food or drink prior to a speaking engagement.

Avoid cold food or drinks. The coldness can affect your vocal cords and even the shaping of your mouth to form words. For this reason, ice-cream is a double whammy. Firstly, it is a phlegm-producing dairy product and secondly, it is a frozen desert that is often presented at meals where the public speaker is about to ply their trade. Awareness and observance are the public speaker's best allies.

What to Wear

Don't wear loud and flamboyant clothing as this may distract the audience from the message that you are trying to convey. Wear clothes that are:

- Suitable to the audience
- Comfortable and practical
- Compliment the topic being presented
- Not a distraction to the audience
- Not sending a message or agenda of some sort

What to Do

Drink room temperature water before speaking. Do not drink large amounts prior to your presentation or you might find that you have to go to the toilet in the middle of your talk. If your throat feels a little dry or scratchy prior to the presentation, then take a half a teaspoon of honey. This will lubricate and sooth your throat.

Wear comfortable clothes and shoes. Prior to your presentation, ensure that you have ascertained the temperature of the room and adjust your clothing needs appropriately. You may be standing on the one spot for the entire duration of your talk so well-supported shoes are imperative.

A little hint that I have learned from the people that stand at attention during military parades is to wiggle and clench your toes inside your shoes, if your shoes have enough room to be able to do that. This will keep the blood circulating. Avoid raising up on your toes or rocking back and forward, as this will most certainly distract from the message you are trying to convey.

I am aware of speakers who use hand movements and subtle shifts of weight on their feet as a stealthy way of circulating as much blood through their systems as they can during a particularly long address. This method, if done right, can enhance a presentation.

Body Language as a Tool of Punctuation

Once a speaker is comfortable with suitable hand, arm and leg movements when presenting, they can now use their body language as a tool to enhance, emphasise and punctuate what is being said.

You can use your arms and hands in fluid motions to help lead from one topic or one sentence to another. For example, use your open right hand in appropriate movement to what you are saying. Close at the end of the topic and bring your arm across your body to your left side where your left hand now opens and takes over the next topic from your right hand. This physically emphasises a change of topic. This can also be achieved by turning your body from one side of the room to another. A small change in body language can enhance a topic by showing a definitive change through slight but effective variation. This is known as the contrast effect.

Nonverbal punctuation can be enhanced further if you align a specific topic with body movements. For example, if you are trying to drive home a serious point to the participants then combine staccato-like speech with a closed fist gently pounding an open palm. Whilst speaking about a soft mellow topic, use your open palms and fingers in a slow fluid motion that mirrors the soft topic. It's like being a well-composed orchestra conductor.

In no way should you over do such a technique. Please ensure that nerves don't have you waving your hands around like you are conducting an orchestra. This is a sure way to distract your audience and ensure that they lose the point of the topic being presented. Body language including micro expressions must match the tone of the topic presented. This may take time to master but it is a valuable presentation tool.

Vocal Exercises

Like any set of muscles in our body, the muscles and tendons that allow us to vocalise need to be warmed up. In our upper arm there are four muscles required to undertake the majority of that limb's requirements. However, speaking requires the use of one hundred muscles. Exercising these muscles is crucial to verbally delivering a message.

There are certain physical and vocal exercises that can be performed to ensure optimum use of our voices when presenting to a group of people.

Mouth exercises can help prepare you vocally for your presentation. The use of exaggerated movement when saying the following words/phrases, will exercise muscles needed for speech and even micro expressions (paralanguage).

If possible, look at yourself in the mirror while doing these exercises to ascertain maximum effective use.

In all these exercises, exaggerate the use of your mouth and jaw while saying and repeating these words and phrases.

These words use different sounds and different breathing patterns. For example, 'Me May More May Moo' use movements and breath to elicit softer, smoother words, whereas 'Tee Tay Tar' use movement to elicit sharper more defined words. It is also advised to use exaggerated breath expulsion to emphasise the sounds and movements you are hoping to make.

It is recommended that these exercises be done as soon as possible before a speaking engagement. Even when moving towards your point of delivery you can be silently mouthing these exercises. It is also recommended that these exercises be repeated at least five times each before a presentation.

At times, circumstances do not allow a presenter to vocalise these mouth exercises. It is acceptable to just mouth the routine without any voice projection.

- Wow
- Me May More May Moo
- Tee Tay Tar
- Flip Flop Flip Flop
- Bee Bow Bee Bow
- Tick Tock Tick Tock

Project Your Voice

Always check unassisted acoustics. Without any microphone assistance it is still possible for your voice to reach those who need to hear it at the majority of venues. Body positioning is vital to being able to be heard at the back of a room of just about any size. Once you have ascertained your scope of delivery (the furthest left participant and the furthest right participant), ensure that you do not project (speak) outside that scope range. Keep your body posture straight and ensure when speaking you can imagine that your chin is pointing to the people in the back row of the classroom, auditorium or conference hall.

Help Them Hear You

Speak clearly and deliberately with even volume, pace and tone with the use of conversational oscillation. Conversational oscillation is where you speak the same way that you would if you were speaking to a friend or relative without the annoying, repetitious peaks and troughs consistent with nervousness or topic unfamiliarity.

If you can, get someone to check your volume and clarity both assisted and unassisted. Get them to roam around the room or auditorium while you read aloud from your delivery station. Be mindful that sound in a room void of people will carry a lot further than sound in a full room. Take that into consideration when finding your appropriate volume. Customise your volume and tone to suit:

- The environment
- The topic
- The participants

Tone is an effective tool. Generally, the lower the tone of your voice the louder you will need to speak. The higher your tone, the further voice will carry. A happy middle tone is best. This is of course when your speaking is unassisted by electronic means.

One of the major problems with public speaking is variation of oral factors, such as pitch, tone, volume and inflection. These variations can be due to several key reasons like internal or external distractions and failure of sound equipment. However, the main reason seems to be unfamiliarity or memory loss relating to topic content.

It is natural to be nervous when you are speaking in front of a group of strangers. This is magnified if you're not familiar with or have forgotten key points of your topic. When this happens the speaker will often lose confidence with what they are saying, and this can result in disjointed thoughts and speech. Volume and tone variations can occur as well, resulting in a usually softer and more high-pitched presentation.

Nerves and How to Beat Them

Nerves can either be your best friend or your worst enemy. Use your nerves and anxiousness as a tool to present better.

As an ally, your nervousness will ensure that you have done your homework and learned your topic well before the day of presentation.

It will ensure that you have that extra burst of adrenalin to give you that much needed edge when presenting to a group of people in an effective and professional way. It will help give credit to you, the topic you are presenting and the organisation you represent. It also shows respect to those listening to you.

As an enemy, your nervousness may make you physical ill, cloud your mind and sap topic memory from you.

Your nerves can give you a dry mouth and throat and also give you an annoying stutter that you didn't realise you had. Nervousness can also cause you to become shaky and some people experience nausea, vomiting and dizziness. Some have even passed out prior to or during a form of public speaking.

Before you speak, find your 'point of relaxation'. Some picture an imaginary scene of serenity or recall a happy event. Dwell on those feelings and emotions that instil a sense of peace and relaxation. Then look at your notes or cue cards, taking a last-minute scan of the key points and the overall topic that you wish to present. It is important however, not to go into depth during this review, as too much crammed information may cause confusion and add to anxiety.

Before I am about to speak in public, I briefly study the first point I wish to present. More specifically, my very first words. They may simply be a welcome, an acknowledgement or a summary of what I am about to say. Doing this acts as a prompt to initiate the rest of my presentation. I find it gives me assurance and helps me exhibit an authoritarian presence for the participant.

Drink a small amount of water before you commence speaking. Mouth and throat lubricating sips are more than sufficient. When you reach your delivery point, pause for a few seconds to gather your thoughts. While this pause is occurring, do not look at the participants but instead look at your notes or cue cards. Doing this has a twofold purpose. Firstly, to take full use of an attention-grabbing 'pregnant pause' and secondly to give you settling time to gather your thoughts. Be mindful not to extend that initial silence too long. This may make the participants feel uneasy and may hinder your period of thought gathering before you speak.

One of the best tools for a nervous public speaker is what I call the gathering time or quiet time. This is where the speaker has some time just before their presentation to be alone in a peaceful environment focusing on mental and emotional settling.

Dos and Don'ts Before You Speak

Don't speak when you are overtired or exhausted. Your mind will not be clear, which will impede your ability to recall information. Your words may come across as jumbled, which may give the listener/observer the impression that you are intoxicated or having a major debilitating health issue.

Don't drink alcohol or take drugs prior to any speaking event. Physiologically they can distort your vocal cords to the point of distorting tone, pitch, pace and volume. They can cause slurred speech and mumbling as well as incoherent and distorted dialogue. Cognition can be severely impaired so that important information is forgotten or rendered unintelligible. To some, alcohol and drugs are used as a source of courage and a tool to build self-esteem. To others it can instil a sense of panic, depression and paranoia.

An audience can be extremely discerning and can identify any variation to normal presentation because of external influences. This can lead to disrespect and lack of confidence in the presenter, the topic and the organisation represented by that presenter. Alcohol and drugs end up not being the relaxing sources of 'Dutch courage' that they purport to be. It is a certain way to limit and distort your effectiveness as a facilitator and a way of losing respect and credibility as an adult educator.

Chapter 14

Session Preparation

Never Rely on Memory Alone

> *'Memory is the faculty of the brain by which information is encoded, stored and retrieved when needed. Memory is vital to experiences; it is the retention of information over time for the purpose of influencing future action. If we could not remember past events, we could not learn or develop language, relationships, or personal identity.'*
>
> **Eysenck, 2012**

Our ability to recall information can be hindered or enhanced by several factors. These include both internal and external. External can be things such as noise, flashing lights and distracting movement within our peripheral vision. Internal distractions can be caused by distracting thoughts, preoccupation with a recent issue or event, illness or general poor health, unfamiliarity of the topic to be presented or innate personality or character traits that may hinder our ability to absorb, recall and expound information. This may include innate or developed bias towards the intent of the topic to be presented.

Never rely on memory, especially with an unfamiliar audience or if you are equipped with unfamiliar material. Know your strengths and know your limitations, then match those personal variables with the strengths and weaknesses of your topic, your audience and your venue. A gentle juggling act to maximise knowledge transfer may be required.

One of the worst delivery options is to read extensive notes verbatim. Reading what is written from notes or other written resources directly from the page is unprofessional and is easily received in a negative way by a participant. It gives the participants little confidence in the trainer and will easily lead to the participants becoming bored.

Quoting resources verbatim can be an excellent tool of delivery as it can emphasise an area of topic through formal, written dialogue. Reference material or statistics can emphatically drive a point home; however, always quote the source.

Palm cards emphasise that you should not rely on memory alone, which is one of the major rules of public speaking, whether it is in front of a conference centre full of people or a small classroom of only six participants. A palm card is exactly what it says it is: a small, thin piece of cardboard or paper that fits comfortably and discretely in the palm of your hand. Not hidden but discreetly placed. The palm card can be either lined or unlined and must contain the key elements of your presentation in chronological point form.

It can be assumed that the number of palm cards you use is dependent upon two factors, the first being the length of your presentation and the second being how much information you have retained relating to the topic you are presenting. The greater your familiarity with the topic, the less detail is required on the palm cards. These resources are purely memory prompts. A brief sentence to remind the facilitator of an element or important section to be delivered. To reiterate: learn, know, retain and be able to recall and present any part of the topic/subject you are asked to deliver.

Topic/Subject Review

Each person has a different study method. Some study at night and into the early hours, while others prefer waking early to study before their day begins. Some prefer to repetitiously recite information-laden texts, hoping that a photographic memory will recall the required information as needed.

Others will summarise important elements of topics on paper and recall relevant information, drawing on past texts read, lectures, seminars or workshops attended, as well as practical information gleaned from on the job experience. Some are visual and learn from observation. Others are auditory and learn better from hearing others present. Whatever method you as an individual find the most efficient learning tool, practise it. If one particular method doesn't seem to hold consistency and does not fulfil one's learning needs, then vary it or combine several methods until you find a formula that does work and produces viable recall results.

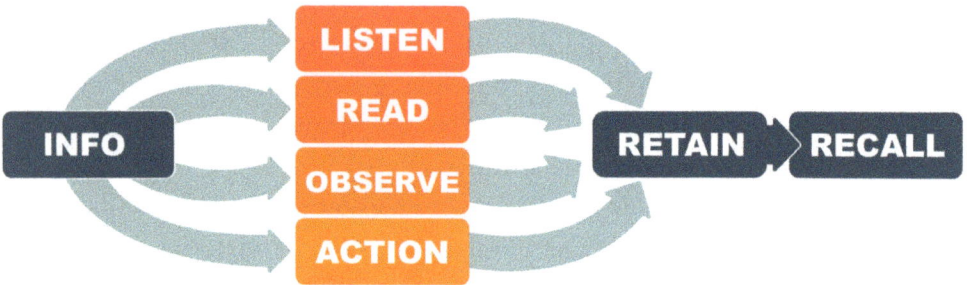

These are important facets of learning that a facilitator/trainer must acknowledge and appreciate when delivering to their audience of students or participants. Each individual in a learning environment has their own style of learning However, in a group environment it is very difficult for the trainer to accommodate those specific learning pathways for every individual present. A trainer, where possible, should incorporate several learning pathways into each presentation. For example, the trainer can use visual stimuli in the form of audio-visual support about a point or topic being presented. Audio recordings can also be used as a tool of support. Verbal or visual reiteration can reinforce to some learners specific, important points. General class discussion can also engage participants to absorb information.

Chapter 15

Emotional Intelligence

A facilitator, presenter, lecturer, guest speaker or any person that delivers a message, subject or topic to a group of people is dealing with multitudes of personalities and personal ideologies that may contrast with the facilitator's own personality traits and ideals.

In most situations, the response to these variations is either to enter into conflict, avoidance or compromise. The response is generally a result of an individual's emotional intelligence (EI) or at what level they can instigate emotional detachment (ED). As a presenter, the latter is seen as a personal attribute that is implemented to avoid unnecessary stress or conflict when a participant or group of participants views clash with their own.

Not all audiences are the same, just as not all presenters are the same. We all have good days and bad days. Our emotions and thought processes for a particular time are governed by many factors, including our health and wellbeing, any negative or positive interactions we may have had preceding our presentations, and any underlying issues that resurface in our consciousness.

The environment that we are about to present in and general state of mind may shape our state of being at any given time. We may be distracted, depressed, angry, or impatient with low tolerance levels at that particular time. How we cope and present ourselves and our material is dependent upon our emotional intelligence and, where appropriate, our emotional detachment.

> *'The ability to be aware of, control, and express one's emotions, and to manage interpersonal relationships judiciously, empathetically and with courtesy.'*
>
> **Daniel Goleman, 2005**

> *'Emotional intelligence is the key to both your personal and professional success and development'*
>
> **David W. Mayne**

Emotional intelligence is being able to identify and manage your own emotions and the ability to recognise and determine the emotions of others that an individual interacts with.

According to Daniel Goleman (2005), an American psychologist who helped to popularise emotional intelligence, there are five key elements pertaining to it:

1. Self-awareness
2. Self-regulation
3. Motivation
4. Empathy
5. Social skills

Self-awareness

Knowing how your actions, emotions and feelings can impact your personal wellbeing and affect those you are with means that you are self-aware. Self-awareness also means that you are conscious of your personal strengths and weaknesses and how they impact on you and the others you interact with.

Self-regulation

Individuals that possess the ability to regulate their own emotions and actions very rarely make rushed or bad decisions. They are in control and have a greater understanding of others' ability to self-regulate. An individual that has elevated self-regulation skills will also understands their own personal triggers that may induce an emotional response. Having a greater awareness of their beliefs, values and what they hold as important, self-regulating individuals will also have practised strategies to cope with stressful or challenging situations.

Motivation

Those with high self-motivation are inspired by their own goals and objectives and will consistently work towards achieving those goals to a high standard. Your own level of self-motivation may equip you to motivate others and encourage them to seek their personal strategies to achieve self-motivation.

In education at any level, it is important that not only you as the facilitator is motivated, but also you transpose that positive motivation to those you hope to educate.

Self-motivation is a continual and developing process. Not only should we use our current long-established skills and strategies to self-motivate but also be open to developing new methods to be used in self-motivation. An individual who has a high level of self-motivation is better equipped to encourage others to raise their own level of self-motivation.

Empathy

Empathy is the ability to observe, listen and emotionally understand how others feel and interpret things.

For presenters, having empathy is critical to maintaining a successful group of learners. Presenters with empathy have the ability to put themselves in someone else's shoes. They help develop the learner in their group, challenge others who are acting unfairly, give constructive feedback, and listen to those who need it.

Pay attention to body language. Perhaps when you listen to someone, you cross your arms, move your feet back and forth, or bite your lip. This body language tells others how you really feel about a situation, and the message you're giving isn't positive! Learning to read body language can be a real asset in a leadership role, because you'll be better able to determine how someone truly feels. This gives you the opportunity to respond appropriately. See Chapter 17 for further information.

Social Skills

Those individuals that are great communicators generally have a high level of social skill and are easily able to adapt to various social situations.

Educators who have high social skills are seen as great communicators. This manifests in a learning environment as open communication and potentially getting the best productivity and engagement from participants.

In education environments, facilitators who possess and display good social skills can also manage change and have a good grasp of resolving conflict. They also have discernment in determining personality and character and how that may reflect a participant's motives or agenda.

Response and Reactions

Newton's third law of physics dictates that for every action there is an equal and opposite reaction. It is often the same when our actions or words are based on emotions and not sound reasoning or logic. Depending on the situation, issues and individuals involved, actions may elicit positive or negative responses or reactions.

- Contemplate your reactions: Exercise your self-awareness to evaluate and adjust your own emotions and the corresponding reactions to those emotions.

Weigh up the positives and negatives of not only your emotions but how those emotions are expressed in actions and words. Individuals that do not have checks and balances with their own emotions are more likely to react negatively in stressful situations.

- See situations as challenges, not setbacks: If you see negative emotional responses in yourself then you are more likely to see negative emotional responses in others. Emotional intelligence is not an exact science and we often perceive our shortcomings in this area as failure, but in fact it is a positive opportunity for growth and development. Setbacks in emotional intelligence are actually challenges that help an individual to increase their skills and strategies for the future.

- Change and adapt your emotions: Those who have emotional intelligence have a greater ability to control their emotions. It is important for an individual to find the balance between excessive anxiety and none at all. This can determine cognitive development, achievement or cognitive deficits. After spending many years working as an educator within correctional facilities, I have seen many inmates adjust and even completely change their emotions and how they respond to them. This empowers them to observe and determine the emotions and responses of others in the facility. In all honesty, some of the most emotionally intelligent people I have ever met have been long term incarcerated. I have had the privilege over the years to watch this metamorphic change and adaptation within at times a very difficult and stressful environment.

- Use of empathy: A high level of emotional intelligence is displayed when an individual makes an effort to understand thoughts and emotions of others. As humans, we react in different ways in different circumstances. An individual with high emotional intelligence will perceive and recognise other stressed individuals and the emotional adjustments they might make in certain situations. It is important to understand why they have reacted that way. This gives you a greater understanding of that person and what events or situations may change their emotional and actioned responses.

Emotions are Not Fixed

All these factors are why workplace emotional intelligence training is now common, with the most effective training focusing on management and expression of emotions, which are directly linked to communication and job performance.

It's also worth pointing out that emotional intelligence is a cognitive ability that can improve across your lifespan. If you haven't recognised much of yourself in the traits listed above, don't be too concerned. There's still time for you to work on your emotional intelligence.

Having a high level of emotional intelligence can determine how you behave in different scenarios or social interactions. It is a tool of personal understanding that helps us to have greater insight into our own self-awareness enabling us to recognise emotions in ourselves and respond appropriately and recognise the emotions and response to emotions in others.

In short, recognising and managing your own emotions and recognising and responding to the emotions of others is demonstrating emotional intelligence.

Chapter 16

Emotional Detachment

Emotional detachment is an unwillingness to relate with others on an emotional plane. These individuals may also not be able to relate to others emotionally. This inability or unwillingness could aid in self-protection against an unwanted drama or stress. For some, detachment isn't always a premeditated choice. It may be a result of events that make an individual not able to be open and honest about their emotions.

The avoidance of emotional connection is known as emotional detachment. It may be a temporary reaction to highly emotional circumstances or a chronic condition such as a depersonalization disorder.

Benefits of Emotional Detachment

To be in a state of emotional detachment is the ability for an individual to separate their emotions from an emotional or potentially emotional situation such as a person who trains themselves to ignore the pleading food requests of a dieting spouse, or indifference by parents towards a child's begging.

Emotional detachment can be seen as positive personal tool that displays a high level of emotional intelligence. It allows a person to distance themselves in a healthy way from highly emotional and negative circumstances. It is a conscious decision by an individual to separate or disengage their emotional response from an actual event or situation that may normally produce a negative and detrimental emotional response. This choice to emotionally disengage could be in personal, social or professional context. Emotionally detaching or disengaging allows an individual to keep personal or professional boundaries. This means that an individual's integrity is not compromised.

Emotional detachment allows an individual to exercise a more astute and well-reasoned empathy towards others without the distortion that emotions sometimes bring to a situation. It allows for well-reasoned thought and provides a defence against being emotionally manipulated by others.

This detachment can be a vital tool in the adult education environment when dealing with potentially difficult participants that may demonstrate disruption or focus on continually portraying a negative mindset in and around the learning environment. In these circumstances, it is important to detach from the potential emotional negativity and focus on the group of participants as a whole.

In a vocational education environment, the need for emotional detachment may occur when a topic elicits an emotional response. Obvious displays of emotion may detract from a professional response. Another would be when an individual or group of participants become angry, emotional and potentially aggressive during a session (this may or may not have any relationship to the topic presented). To mirror negative behaviour as a figure of authority may give support or credence to this behaviour. Taking a neutral or detached position may well subdue or neutralise the situation.

Possible Disadvantages of Emotional Detachment

There is a negative side to emotional detachment. Emotional numbing can become an innate behaviour of chronic dissociation and depersonalisation that may lead to a depersonalisation disorder. This manifests as a complete disconnection from emotion described as emotional blunting or numbing. This complete emotional dissociation is viewed in severe trauma situations as a coping mechanism however, over time it becomes a chronic day to day method for an individual to deal with stress.

History has taught that emotional detachment may evolve (although rarely) into a characteristic for an individual to allow cruelty and abuse, showing little empathy for others and leading to antisocial behaviours.

In the education sector, it is important to focus on the course, subject or topic to be delivered, as well as the participants. However, over a period of regular face-to-face contact with participants it is human nature to form attachments and make personal assessments about a participant or several participants. As an unbiased facilitator, it is mandatory that you separate your feelings, judgements, and determinations about the participants. You must never allow your personal thoughts and feelings to cloud, distort or distract you from your commissioned task of imparting knowledge, experience or skills to the participants.

It is important that this ability to detach emotionally from individuals does not become ingrained or an innate state of being that impacts on you personally.

Emotional detachment can sometimes appear as a negative coping mechanism and it is important to recognize the signs when it becomes problematic. This means that the personal and emotional detachment you have in the education/professional environment should not transpose to your personal environment. The skill is not so much being able to detach; the real skill is knowing when to.

In your personal world, detachment may at times negatively affect relationships. If you feel that your workplace detachment protocols are encroaching into your personal world, then perhaps external support, such as therapy, may be beneficial. This may help you to develop strategies to be able to determine when to use emotional detachment and when not to.

Many occupations, such as front-line medical services, that deal directly with others in highly stressful and emotive situations learn to be able to detach themselves appropriately. This, for some, does not come easily and requires personal conditioning to equip them with the strategies and tools to make the smooth transitions required between emotional detachment and emotional attachment. This does not mean that you must take on the persona of a heartless robot in front of participants, but through emotional intelligence and your own self-awareness, you should be more cognizant of how to separate personal and emotive responses from professional duty of care in the education sector.

This is an acquired skill that is not to be feared but seen as an important tool to use in certain educational environments, equipping you to better fulfill your roles and responsibilities of a facilitator.

Chapter 17

Dealing with Difficult Participants or Groups

'Show respect even to people who don't deserve it; not as a reflection of their character, but as a reflection of yours.'

Dave Willis, 2017

As human beings, we express ourselves through our personality and character as well as things such as genetics, gender, mood and wellbeing. This shows others who we are.

The Family

Who we are is a product of many elements, like our parents, their parenting styles and their individual influences as a couple. Parents and siblings are present in our formative years, becoming important influences on us. In the early years of our lives, they give us templates that we mould ourselves on. We see our immediate family's behaviours and hear their words, and through trust and familiarity we come to believe their behaviours to be correct, leading to emulation. This is for better or worse. As we grow, other individuals or groups may influence us and some of those influences may contradict or even be diametrically opposed to those beliefs instilled in us by our parents or siblings. These conflicting views may cause agitation, frustration and confusion as we get older and the expression of these emotions privately or in public may be deemed antisocial, antiauthority or antiestablishment. This is where self-awareness and emotional intelligence are vital as an individual determines their own ongoing development of character, personality and behaviours.

In multi-sibling families, birth order can have a profound influence when examining our position within the family unit. It can affect where we fit into society and how we express personal developments socially, at school or the workplace. This may adjust as we get older, gain experience and are influenced by others with their own paradigms.

Education

Our education, from kindergarten to postdoctoral, shapes us throughout our life. Input of ideas during this period is directly from and controlled by teachers and lecturers. Sometimes these ideas are coloured by the opinions, ideologies and prejudices of those same instructors.

As well as the instructors in our educational years, there are fellow students/peers that bring a potential myriad of different thoughts, behaviours and ideals to our lives. Over time, some of these thoughts may influence, revaluate or even change your own thoughts, behaviours and ideals.

Friends and workplace peers who we interact with socially and professionally reflect their own set of ideals and influences. This can happen over time as familiarity and trust grows. When shown respect, there is a greater chance of an individual listening to and receiving another person's ideals and thoughts and giving credence and validity to those opinions or behaviours.

Geography

Where we grew up can have an enormous influence on who we are as people. The relative isolation of a farm in regional areas compared to a populous city can determine huge behavioural differences relating to interaction with others. This can include shyness or overfamiliarity as well as many other interpersonal social interactions that have been determined on where we were born and where we grew up.

The country we are born and raised in influences us through that country's cultural, educational and religious practises. If you doubt this, then research the number of wars and conflicts that have occurred because of a clash of ideals based on culture or religion. These clashes are sometimes mirrored at local grass roots and personal levels.

Physical Wellbeing and Mental Health

A sickness or disability, either long-term or recently acquired, can have a huge impact on who we are and how we perceive the world and those around us. If in illness you are in constant or managed pain, you may express your thoughts and ideas in a certain way as you do in accepting others thoughts and ideals. Cognition, mental health and physical impairment can dictate how we can both receive information and express our own information to others. Medication may enhance or hinder a person's ability to receive, understand and recall information. Physical and emotional trauma impacts on concentration and information retention. For example, the symptoms of post-traumatic stress disorder (PTSD) can severely impede and individual in a learning environment.

Bias

Preconceptions and prejudices that have been instilled in us over our formative years and beyond shape how we react and respond when placed in an environment or situation where these ideas are challenged. An individual may have a very narrow conception of a certain world view, but this is because of the influences ingrained throughout their life, pre or post the informative years. These views may be frowned upon by the majority of society today; however, we may not be aware of the experiences that have shaped that individual into thinking and feeling that their views and attitudes are correct and valid. By judging that person instead of understanding them and what influences have affected their lives, we may fall into the same trap of being judgmental and opinionated based on self-righteousness and ignorance.

Phobias

Phobias and innate fears can be very debilitating to an individual and limit their ability to use logic and reason to overcome them. These phobias may well be brought into the learning facility by participants. Statistics say that a large percentage of participants have some sort of phobia and some have fears and anxiety triggered by certain external stimuli. Research states that 10% of individuals have a phobia of some sort.

Handling Negative Behaviours

All these elements shape who we are and how we present and express ourselves to others. This can have a huge influence on not only what information we hope to present and how it is presented, but also how it is listened to, accepted and retained by participants in a learning environment.

In understanding and acknowledging the external and internal catalysts that shape us as people and facilitators, it is also vitally important that we understand and acknowledge that our participants and audiences have had their own life journeys that have shaped who they are when they sit down in front of you. The huge disadvantage that you have as a facilitator is the fact that there is a high probability that you don't know any of these people or what shaped them into who they are now.

It is your job as a facilitator about to transfer your topic through knowledge, experience and study, that you to find a neutral delivery method for the knowledge, skills and experience you wish to impart.

As presenters we must accept that the people in front of us all have different lives shaped by different experiences that may or may not impede their ability to learn and retain knowledge. Interpersonal skills including social interaction may be presented at various levels. As a facilitator, you must rely on initial observation and brief interactions, both verbal and nonverbal, to determine if an individual displays issues that may be disruptive or distracting to the rest of the participants.

Before participants first enter the room ensure that you are there first. Participants should never enter a room without the facilitator or trainer being in their delivery position. The exception to the rule is when the facilitator or guest speaker is being introduced by a master of ceremonies or a previous speaker. It is respectful if the facilitator/educator is already present in the venue when the participants start to arrive. When they start to walk in and before they take a seat, observe if they walk in alone, with a friend or in with someone they may have only just met. Observe any eye contact with yourself or with others. Look for cursory greetings like a quick 'hello' or just a nod of acknowledgement.

Depending on the seating configuration of the room, observe where participants sit and if that seat was predetermined or randomly selected by the participant. It is common that on the first day of a class, seminar or one-day workshop that most participants will try and sit in an inconspicuous location, usually at the back or side of a room. This is normal and should not be taken as sign that that participant is evasive or reserved. It is likely first-day nerves.

Watch for those rarer participants that make a beeline for the seat at the front-middle, closest to the facilitator. It is a good idea to consider why that person sat there. Perhaps eyesight or hearing difficulties. Perhaps sitting there helps them concentrate and improves cognitive receptibility. The other reason could be as a form of misguided intimidation towards the facilitator. Perhaps they are there under duress; a directive from their workplace or an employment agency. It could be in defiance, as they feel that they know as much or more about the topic/course than the facilitator does, and they want the opportunity to show off to the other participants. It could be a form of overcompensation for a low self-esteem. That person may have no gripe against you or the course, or maybe they do! You don't know their headspace at that time or what happened in their lives leading up to that behaviour.

It should also be noted that as humans we are not expected to get along with everyone we meet on life's journey, and this goes for those in a trainer-student relationship in adult education. There will often be those who have opposing views that we need to interact with either socially or professionally. Although it can be personally frustrating, confronting and even demeaning, it is important that we remain neutral and non-disclosive of our own world views, including religious and political beliefs and other potentially contentious or divisive ideals.

Some participants may slip out of their normal personal demeanour and become talkative, loud, confrontational or aggressive. This is a nervous reaction and is generally the opposite of how they are in their day-to-day life. Hopefully this is a temporary state of being until they find their place in the class meet others, thus letting the nerves settle down through course and facilitator familiarity.

It is important not to enter a confrontation or other verbal exchange with people who exhibit negative behaviour. As a facilitator, you're not aware of the history of that participant or any underlying issues that have caused that participant to express themselves in a particular way. If the individual directly confronts you with sarcastic or competitive comments in front of other participants, do not retort by entering debate or any discussion. Advise the participant that you would prefer to talk with them after the session has finished. As the motive or agenda of that participant is unknown, it is advisable to conduct that discussion within the venue privately, where you are possibly under some form of video surveillance. Alternatively, conduct the discussion within easy hearing of other staff members. As you are unfamiliar with that participant or potential reactions, it is advisable that you are in a professionally public area as a form of subtle security.

When you feel secure, initially allow the agitated participant to talk or vent about what was concerning them during the delivery session. Use affirming and attentive body language and use minimal verbal responses. However, during this time carefully observe that participant's own body language, eye contact and the tone, pitch and volume of their voice. Erratic eye movement with no fixed target as well as fast-talking, high-pitched speech indicates that the participant is agitated, frustrated and potentially aggressive. The most effective way of dealing with someone with possible irrational, negative behaviour is to remain calm, say very little but show attentive and positive demeanour toward the participant. This is the 'mirroring affect', a conflict resolution technique where one participant takes the passive role, exhibiting calming body language such as slow hand and arm movements, open positioning shoulders, and varying eye contact. Remember that fixed eye contact may be confronting to the agitated participant and may even escalate their behaviour. Keep your voice even, slow and low volume. If you maintain this persona for a few minutes this can have a calming effect on the agitated participant and they gradually mirror the facilitator's demeanour, diffusing the situation.

When the participant has reached a calm level, maintain your relaxed demeanour and then ascertain the cause of that participant's aggression. If you notice that the participant's agitation is returning, withdraw discussion and re-establish calming speech and body language until the participant is once again calm. Then recommence discussion.

Deal first with the issues that are presented, then deal carefully with the negative way that those issues were presented in class as well as in the current private meeting. Always ensure that, if possible, you have positively addressed any issues raised by the participant and have proactive solutions that are acceptable to all involved. Ascertain through discussion and observation if this will be and ongoing scenario with this participant or if this is a one-off incident.

Due to limitations regarding the disclosure of personal details, the facilitator may not be able to ascertain the root cause of this negative behaviour. In this case, the only course of action is to deal with what is presented by the participant and deal with the immediate issues, responding only to what information has been offered by that participant.

If no understanding, resolution or agreement is reached, then a third-party person is engaged as an observer/mediator. In a professional adult education environment, there are designated professionals that act to find conflict resolution. These may be trained councillors or human resource officers. A third-party mediator needs to understand why a resolution cannot be reached between the facilitator and a participant by gathering information from each person separately and then determining an approach to resolution.

After initial resolution management, it is important that a follow-up meeting is undertaken to ascertain if any original issues are still there or if any new or related issues have emerged. At this follow-up meeting, any existing or new issues can be addressed and future follow-up meetings scheduled.

Ideally, conflict or contentious issues should be addressed through face-to-face meetings. Communications such as telephone, email or social media messages lack the ability to observe body language, including micro expressions. This strongly disadvantages both parties in ascertaining meaning and intent of the other person, therefore is a potentially limiting factor in conflict resolution.

Mob Mentality

People form groups for many reasons. It could be like-mindedness, a sporting team, or a class full of students undertaking a stressful course. Unity and bonds often develop. Because of this unity there may be scenarios where individuals participating in the same course empathise with a fellow participant that feels they are being given a hard time by the trainer. As a distraction or eversion to a boring topic or class issue, one disgruntled participant with a collaborating negative view is joined by another agreeing participant, who is then joined by another and another until a mob mentality has developed. Safety and possibly anonymity in numbers. This could be directed at another individual, such as the facilitator or a fellow participant, or at the training body operating that particular education program.

This negative and often disruptive mob dynamic is easy to disperse but may take a little manoeuvring and micro political practices. Find out who the instigator or instigators are and have a private conversation away from the rest of the participants to address the issue or issues. Resolve any problems and ensure that those instigators are now satisfied that issues have been resolved. It is imperative that any disgruntled animosity within the group of participants has been rectified in a positive manner prior to the participants returning to the group. All the while, gather important information about the dissidents in case of future disgruntled behaviour.

In all conflict resolution scenarios ensure that positive outcomes are obtained if possible, ensuring that participants feel what they say is of value and that resolution processes are undertaken in an encouraging, edifying manner.

The aim is that once they key negative class influencers have re-joined the group, the same domino effect will comes into play to rectify at a wider level.

Facilitators should be very discerning regarding a mob issue within a group of participants. In some cases, there may be a valid point where the facilitator has errored in some way, and that needs to be addressed directly by the facilitator towards the general class if applicable. There are times when the mob action is unjustified and the facilitator must be cautious not to take blame and lose confidence through self-flagellation and fear of poor judgement. It may not be your fault and the issues that have arisen through a single disgruntled participant whose misguided focus is directed towards the person of authority in the room. Others who agree with this individual's thinking may have the same or their own reasons for joining the negative mob. They might also see this as a vehicle of distraction from their own poor results or poor attendance. Blaming the facilitator removes the spotlight from them.

'Meekness is not weakness, it is power in control'

David W. Mayne

```
ISSUE / STATEMENT
    ↓           ↓
  REAL        FALSE
    ↓           ↓
  TIME +      TIME +
  GOSSIP      GOSSIP
    ↓           ↓
INCREASE IN  INCREASE IN
DISSENSION   DISSENSION
    ↓           ↓
   FACTUAL DETERMINATION
            ↓
      POSITIVE ACTION
            ↓
        RESOLUTION
```

Anti-Authority

As I have discussed, you will encounter many varying personalities and characters with many varying backgrounds in a group you are facilitating. Some of those people may have acquired a propensity to dislike those in authority and demonstrate that dislike by challenging the authority, belittling the authority or humiliating the authority in front of other participants.

There are times when a facilitator and/or the host training organisation must decide if a participant should remain in the group or be removed. This is a hard decision for any facilitator to make and is a drastic but sometimes necessary course of action. If the participant's behaviour is upsetting and distracting to other participants, or the participant is a physical danger to others, self or property, and attempts to resolves conflict have failed, then the decision must be made to remove that participant from the group. However, this course of action must be seen as a last resort where all avenues of discussion and resolution have failed.

Talkative

There are those people who enjoy talking a lot. There is a myriad of reasons that a person will be more talkative than others. Sometimes it's nerves, shyness or a compensation for a low self-esteem, others are just plain talkative as part of their nature and personality. They are usually upbeat, open and friendly, though at times they can also be overbearing, distracting and exhausting, a time sponge that can dominate discussion and talk over other participants and derail session plans and course objectives.

The best way to deal with a 'have a chat' is to have a plan of moderate inclusion. Engage them initially in general course discussion then ask for other participants' input, even naming another participant to comment about what's being discussed. If the 'have a chat' keeps trying to comment through interjection, gently remind that person that others should have a say as well.

Try not to use phrases like, 'Anyone have any questions or queries?' This is an opening for the 'have a chat'. Be cautious that you don't stifle the 'have a chat' into silence. This is obviously not wanted either. If the overshadowing interjection continues, during a break privately and positively discuss the need for others to have their say but also comment on the importance of that person having a say as well. Even thanking the 'have a chat' for their valuable contribution to class discussion.

Edification of positive input, general class contribution and the need for all participants to feel free to have comment should act as a gentle leveller and empower the 'have a chat' to feel good about other participants having input into discussion as well.

If the constant interjections and dominance of discussion continue, then another private discussion should be had with the 'have a chat' in a firmer more assertive manner. Continue to edify that participant and repeat their importance to the group and how valid their comments are, but state plainly that other participants must have opportunity to have input through their comments as well.

Non-Talkative

For those participants that remain quiet well after the first day jitters, it is important to gently include them in general discussion without spotlighting. Spotlighting is the obvious singling out of an individual in front of other participants. This can be extremely confrontational and embarrassing for the quiet participant. Spotlighting can be even more detrimental to a facilitator's objective of total participant inclusion. Ask open questions requiring more than yes/no answers.

Perhaps ask the quiet participant their opinion rather than a required scholastic answer. If the non-responsiveness continues, consider that they could have some social or cognitive impairment that has not been disclosed during enrolment declarations. Do not ask the participant if they have a non-disclosed issue that may limit their input into class discussion. Instead ask if there is anything you as a facilitator can do to help make the course/session/topic more profitable or inclusive for the participant.

The Know-It-All

The know-it-all is a participant that exclaims publicly that they know the topic being delivered and feels that they are wasting their time being in the course or workshop as they could ably impart the required information themselves. They may have industry or academic experience that gives them knowledge of the topic. During a delivery session, this participant may also add to, or counter information made by the facilitator.

If these disruptive comments become a recurring event, then the facilitator should have a private meeting with the know-it-all. The facilitator should remind them that there are other participants that don't know the topic and that the know-it-all may still learn something, if not from the material provided or the facilitator then from other participants with industry-based knowledge. If the know-it-all continues to be disruptive and divisive, then in another private meeting they may be asked to stop the competitive interjections. If this more assertive approach proves to be unsuccessful then the participant may be asked to leave the course.

Due to disclosure laws and policies of some government bodies and organisations, certain personal conditions or issues of a participant are not declared at enrolment or registration. It is not appropriate to ask a participant if you suspect that they have a condition or issue that may have direct impact on their own learning or the learning of other participants within the group. Instead allow conversation to develop where, through trust and professional familiarity, the participant freely discloses the condition or issue. The facilitator and/or organisation may then enact delivery adjustment to improve the participant's learning experience. This may be through tutorial support or recommended reading and adjusting assessment requirements to better suit the participants needs.

Post-Traumatic Stress Disorder (PTSD)

In adult education this topic has familiar and far to common relevance. I'm sure the incidence or participants with PTSD has always been there however, in modern times, we are more likely to recognise the causes and symptoms in our own lives as well as those we come in contact with.

Over the years I have come in contact with many adults with either declared or potentially undeclared PTSD. One participant in their early fifties had to sit near the door and that door had to remain open while she was inside the room at a session. Another example was in a training room at a hospital where a war veteran was a course participant. Unfortunately, the training room was adjacent to the 'helipad' for the emergency rescue helicopter. The sound of incoming or outgoing helicopters caused this participant to become highly agitated, even to the extent of physical manifestations in the form of cold sweats, uncontrolled shaking and nausea.

This section is about awareness and recognition not as a strategy to remedy.

Generally, a trainer or facilitator is not a psychologist and they should in no way determine or make a pseudo-diagnosis on the condition or issue of an individual. However, a knowledgeable observation may give broad insight into a person's behaviour. These unsubstantiated judgements are for the facilitator only, to help them gain possible knowledge relating to a participant's behaviour. This knowledge may or may not be correct, so cannot be thought of as an accurate summation of an individual's behaviour but a broad guideline of possible understanding. As a facilitator can only make personal determinations on the behaviours presented by the participant, often unsubstantiated determination through observation.

Symptoms of PTSD may present from a single traumatic event or the culmination of many negative traumatic inputs over a period of time.

As an adult educator of many years, I have encountered several examples of PTSD and its influences and manifestations in the education environment.

When presenting to adults that have already had many varied and at times traumatic life experiences, it is expected that situations can occur where an individual participant manifests and expresses reactions to PTSD in the learning environment. This may be a serving army veteran who fears loud sudden noises, an abuse victim who needs to sit near the exit and never has the door closed, or a car accident trauma sufferer who breaks into a cold sweat and shakes uncontrollably at the sound of traffic and sirens. A World Health Organisation (WHO) study in 2023 estimated that 3.6% of the world population experienced PTSD in a given year. In any given year, about 5 in every 100 adults will have PTSD. The WHO releases guidance on mental health care after trauma.

- 6% of people ages 18-29 had PTSD sometime in their life.
- 8% of people ages 30-44 had PTSD sometime in their life.
- 9% of people ages 45-59 had PTSD sometime in their life.

(World Health Organization, 2023)

The age demographics match those seeking and undertaking adult education.

Caused by physical, emotional, or psychological trauma, post-traumatic stress disorder (PTSD) is a mental health condition. It can be triggered by an individual being involved or witnessing a terrifying or horrendous event. Years later the individual may experience nightmares, flashback memories, anxiety and even physical manifestations such as shaking, cold sweats, syncope and irrational fits of rage. An individual who suffers from PTSD may have little control over the symptoms and reactions, sometimes having a relived experience that is just as real to them many years later as it was at the time of the trauma event.

PTSD symptoms can vary in intensity over time. You may have more PTSD symptoms when you're stressed in general, or when you come across reminders of what you went through. For example, you may hear a car backfire and relive combat experiences. Or you may see a report on the news about a sexual assault and feel overcome by memories of your own assault (Mayo Clinic USA, 2018).

A large proportion of people experience traumatic events in some form throughout their lives however, they may only experience symptoms for a short time. Self-management and external counselling may lessen the symptoms. With others, it can be a day-to-day way of life and coping mechanisms are not enough to lessen the symptoms.

It is important to note that PTSD symptoms can vary in severity and that can change over a period for an individual. Apart from intrusive memories, negative mood changes and physical reactions can be primary symptoms, as is avoidance.

It is not mandatory that an individual will declare to a learning institution that they suffer from PTSD. However, it is important for an educator to observe an individual's presented symptoms and act on any negative impact that those symptoms have on the individual and others present in a learning environment. This could mean offering support or help to the PTSD sufferer by a qualified practitioner or engage with the individuals already established support.

Untruths and Distorted or Created Realities

Sadly, professionally and socially we encounter those people who tell untruths for personal gain, avoidance or protection. There are those people to whom lying is normality and they rely on untruths to get by socially and professionally. They are found in the sphere of adult education too. These people may be compulsive or habitual liars. For some people, lying is a part of their very being. Their lies are so convincing that they fool themselves and the lies become truth, imbedded in their reality. The following is a brief summary of five types of liars a trainer/facilitator may engage with as a participant or even peer.

Sociopathic Liars

Individuals who lie continually to get what they want without caring about others and the affect they have on others are sociopathic liars. These individuals focus on their own agendas and goals. Achieving these goals is of fundamental importance to the sociopathic liar. This can be at the expense of personal and professional relationships. They are often outgoing, personable with an apparent charm. These seemingly charismatic individuals are self-centred and manipulative.

Compulsive or Pathological Liars

Individuals that have developed a habit of lying are compulsive liars. They are also called habitual or pathological liars. They are comfortable in lying and it is their normal practice. Telling the truth makes them uneasy as if it opens them up to vulnerability. Telling lies makes them comfortable and somewhat at ease.

A primary characteristic of the compulsive liar is their need to bend and manipulate the truth. Apart from habit, a compulsive liar will lie as it is an easier mode of behaviour than if they have to face the truths of their personal undesirable reality.

> *'Lying seems to empower them. They gain power and gratification at being able to create a false reality that they think deceives others.'*
>
> **David W. Mayne (2020)**

Possibly manifested in childhood years, the behaviour of a compulsive liar impinges greatly on personal and professional relationships. This includes all speres of education from early childhood, academia to later in life adult education.

Occasional Liars

Individuals that seldom tell a lie are described as occasional liars. On the rare occasion when they do lie, they feel guilty in doing so and display that guilt in their nonverbal body language. They are also very repentant for their lie and seek restitution.

Careless Liars

Liars that have not really planned or thought out their lie are considered careless liars. They don't try and hide their lie and may display a laisser-faire attitude if found out. This attitude of seemingly benign lying often results in the careless liar not having many friends or work associates, as fellow participants and presenters often tire of hearing exaggerated facts and untruths.

White Liars

Those individuals who tell white lies do not see themselves as liars, instead they feel that a harmless lie may eventually work for good or even a productive, positive result. They often tell part-truths to help cover up or give validity to the adjoining lie. They may have a good agenda or motive for telling a white lie for fear of hurting another person with potentially damaging reality.

Sadly, lying is common in our professional and personal lives, and this includes adult education environments. It is however, beneficial to observe and identify the liar in a learning environment to help protect the individual and others in that environment.

> *'Put some truth in every lie to tickle itching ears.'*
>
> **2 Timothy 4:3**

Be cautious of falling into the role of armchair-psychologist in the learning environment. This information is to give the facilitator knowledge and insight only into potential adverse behaviour by the participant. This in no way equips the facilitator as a specialist clinician.

Identifying a liar in an adult education environment is an important facet of observation. A confirmed observation will go a long way to planning a strategy to deal with the liar. The majority of lies participants tell are simple excuses for an inability to meet a required target such as, 'I lost my assignment', 'my printer broke', 'I was late for the session because my car broke down' or 'my Grandmother died'. Calling the participant on these white lies may be detrimental when it comes to the big picture success of that participant completing a course or a session. If the lies become a frequent habit or become more intense and detailed, then the participant may need to have their possible falsehoods discussed and addressed.

In most situations, if a person is called out on a lie, they will cover up with another lie. The participant may accept that they have been called out as a liar and move on or cease to lie altogether.

It is imperative in an adult learning environment that any conflict or sign of developing conflict between any combination of participants, facilitators or ancillary staff is identified, understood, and rectifying strategies are put in place as soon as possible. Conflict needs to be dealt with immediately. Failure to do so may cause the conflict to escalate unnecessarily to a point that substantial effort and time may be needed to rectify the situation. If not addressed, the conflict may not be able to be resolved at all. People face/deal with conflict in different ways. This is governed by the individual's personality, character, history and how they have been able to deal with conflict in previous situations as well as the conflict at hand. Procrastination over a conflict is not conducive to a resolution.

Argumentative People

Some participants may feel the need to always challenge a facilitator either professionally or personally. This may be the need of one-upmanship or may be a personality trait of the participant. As a facilitator, never be baited into adverse discussion or confrontation with that participant, especially in a public environment with other participants or staff present. This is highly unprofessional and not conducive to a harmonious learning environment.

If the argumentative statements continue in front of other participants or during a delivery session, then speak to the participant privately and ask why that participant is displaying antagonistic behaviour towards the presenter.

Avoid an argument and deal with issues and statements, not emotions and suppositions. If the adverse behaviour continues then a more assertive approach may be necessary, potentially with a third person involved. If a resolution is not achieved and the argumentative comments continue, then the participant may have to be moved to another group or leave the training all together.

Rude, Obscene, Sexist and Racist Comments

During a course, seminar, or workshop, participants may make rude, obscene or discriminatory comments. This is never acceptable, no matter what the root cause or reason for the comment. If the participant states an unacceptable comment publicly during a session, then the facilitator should quickly state in a calm non-confrontational manner that this type of comment is unacceptable in that particular learning environment and there may be people present who could find such comments offensive.

People are entitled to their own opinions based on their own ideals and past experiences. However, there are many who do not share those same views. A closed learning environment is not the place to expound contentious ideologies. Someone is sure to be offended. Even if the facilitator/trainer is in agreement with what the participant said, they are not to give that comment credence or affirm the participant for saying it.

If the comments continue, then a private meeting between the participant and the facilitator may be required to make perfectly clear to the participant that their comments are offensive and not conducive to a harmonious learning environment.

Do not tell the participant that you agree with their beliefs or ideologies. This may be raised by the participant with other participants as a form of showing peers that participant has authority support. The safe position for both participants and facilitators when you are thinking of saying something potentially contentious or inflammatory is, 'When in doubt … don't.'

Reluctant Participants

There will always be those participants who are in attendance against their will or desire to be somewhere else. They are present to fulfil a wish or directive from somebody or somewhere else, such as a workplace initiative or directive, a promotional requirement or a disciplinary directive related to a workplace infringement.

They could be there for a required training course from an employment services organisation, increasing their employability potential and adding greater value to a resume. The participant may also be present at the training as a mandatory court directive or as part of a community service program.

Participants may also be present as a directive from an employment services organisation that the participant has registered with.

It is easy to identify individuals who are participating in training under duress. These people will sit as far away from the presenter and other participants as possible. They would have brought nothing with them in the way of pens or paper. Their body language will be closed with no or very little eye contact and they will speak in monosyllabic responses. They will be late arrivals and will often give drawn-out reasons to why they need to leave early. Many times, they will not turn up at all or will leave early, as they think simply showing their face will appease the person or organisation that has mandated the training as evidence of attendance.

During sessions they may exhibit apathy and disinterest or become disruptive and antagonistic towards the facilitator or other participants. This is a form or rebellion against the establishment.

That establishment can be legal authorities, workplace management or employment agencies that mandated their course attendance. Sadly, that rebellion can manifest itself inside a training facility during a session.

How to Engage the Disgruntled, Disengaged and Disruptive Participant

A facilitator must identify a non-cooperative and disinterested individual, find out the reason for their presence at the training, then determine how their disinterest manifests during a session. Once these factors have been discerned, it is imperative for the trainer to act quickly and efficiently to attend to the disruptive individuals and the issues presented by them.

If the participant is displaying quiet, unobtrusive disinterest that has little or no impact on the session or other participants, it is an issue of that individual's motivation and course or class engagement. Outside a delivery session, have an informal discussion with that participant and steer the conversation as to why they are at the training. Allow them to tell you why they do not want to be there. Once full disclosure is obtained, formulate a collaborative plan to address the situation.

Identify the positive elements of the course and the desirable outcomes of completion such as a qualification, acquired skills and knowledge, potential increase in salary, and gaining valuable experience and practical information.

Relate these positive benefits directly to the individual as an employee, job or promotion seeker or as someone trying to fulfil a judicial mandate or court directive. Focus on the positive outcomes of being an engaged participant and try to convince the individual that they can also have positive and beneficial contributions in the sessions, contributing to the positive outcomes for others.

During this initial discussion, evaluate through listening and observing whether the participant is actively listening to you and participating in the conversation, and if they are responding to you in a positive way or just supplying the answers that they think you want to hear.

During this discussion ensure that you as facilitator maintain a quiet and open demeanour. Don't speak to much. Spend more time listening to the other person, affirming what they say through positive body language and encouraging facial expressions.

If the individual blocks discussion with you and reiterates the reasons why they don't want to undertake the training, indicating that they will continue this apathetic attitude, then you may need to remind them of the reason they are there in the first place. If you still get an indifferent attitude, then you may need to inform them that you will notify the organisation or individual that mandated their attendance of their negative behaviour.

If they have enrolled under their own volition and are still disengaged then you need to inform them that it is not compulsory that they attend and should either engage and find new motivation based on the original reasons for enrolling, or discontinue as a participant.

If the participant is apathetic and disengaged towards the training and is also disruptive within a session and towards the facilitator and/or other participants, then a private informal discussion should also be undertaken. The facilitator's, other participants' and possibly the training organisation's concerns should be presented to the individual. During this discussion, a firmer and more direct approach may be required. The facilitator as the authority within the training organisation, should lead the discussion. It is advisable that a person with more authority within the training organisation does not chair this meeting, as this could be viewed as 'ganging up' on the participant. This may escalate some form or aggressive or antagonistic behaviour and nullify any rectification process.

During this frank discussion, mention that the disruptions the individual is making are having a direct and detrimental impact upon others at the training sessions. Quote complaints you may have received, both written and verbal, making sure to keep complainants anonymous.

At this point reiterate that you would like the participant to remain in the class and hopefully benefit from the training. Ask them if there is a reason that they are behaving in this negative and disruptive manner. If no adequate response is given, do not immediately inform the participant that they will have to leave the course but give a set time period (two days for example) to think about their situation at the training course. Inform them that the training organisation will be contacting them at the end of that period to ascertain if they wish to continue with the training.

Experience has often shown an individual presented with this option will do personal revaluation and return as a valuable participant or agree to leave the course of training. Occasionally, participants will desert the course and be discontinued by the training organisation through enrolment termination. This discontinuation must occur after sufficient, direct, verbal and written warnings have been given.

Dropped the Ball

If an engaged participant suddenly shows signs of disengagement or distress, then an informal discussion with the participant should be undertaken.

Ask the participant what you as the trainer/facilitator or the training organisation can do to support the participant, if that is what has been alluded to by the participant. This often requires a referral to an external organisation that specialises in the issues presented by the participant. These issues may be personal or professional but it is recommended to utilise a third party to help.

Questions Not to Ask

In any discussions that you have with a participant, it is imperative, both privately or in a class situation, that you do not ask personal or leading questions of the participant to investigate why they seem to be disengaged recently. Do not ask questions such as:

- Is everything alright at home?
- Do you have relationship issues?
- How is your health?
- Do you have a drug or alcohol problems?

Asking these sorts of questions to any disengaged participant may be seen as intrusive, demeaning, invasive and crossing personal boundaries. If the participant offers information freely then that is a different matter; however, the facilitator must not offer the participant advice or direction if the area of disclosed concern is out of the facilitator's scope of experience. Guidance should handled by external bodies that may be able to help the individual in a specific and professional way.

It is crucial that the facilitator shows empathy through brief affirming comments and open body language during any communication.

Drugs and Alcohol

Prescription

Each participant should be advised by their physician to declare any medication prescribed to them at enrolment but only if it may affect them physically or cognitively. This does not mean that the participant is obligated to disclose medications. It is a conscious decision by the individual participant if they wish to disclose.

From the facilitator/trainer's point of view, it only becomes an issue if the participant exhibits behaviour that is non-conducive to an appropriate and productive learning environment. This may include disruptive or aggressive behaviour, lethargy and sleepiness or others behaviours associated with the participant's physical or psychological condition.

If the participant's condition and medication is declared on the enrolment form, then the trainer and/or training organisation representative can inquire about the participant's wellbeing, bringing to their attention any observed negative behaviour. Their response will determine how you will deal with the situation and what strategy you will use. If the participant is unaware or consciously unable to realise their negative impact on the training environment, then any next-of-kin or carer contacts declared on the participant's enrolment form should be contacted for confidential advice on the best way to handle the situation, giving utmost respect to the participant.

Non-prescription

In some cases, non-prescription drugs are illegal and may illicit unpredictable and at times adverse behaviour in the user. This may include disruptive and aggressive behaviour as well as lethargy and sleepiness.

As a trainer, you can only enquire to the actions/behaviour presented by the participant at a particular time or continually over a period of time. If the participant's behaviour causes disruption within the training environment, then this needs to be addressed directly with that participant and they must be made aware of the adverse impact they are having on others. A positive slant would be to enquire as to how the trainer/facilitator or training organisation may be of assistance to the participant.

Offer relevant internal or external services to help that participant gain the most out of the enrolled training. If the participant is not willing to acknowledge an issue, or unable to perceive one exists, then if a next-of-kin has been nominated on the enrolment form, they can be contacted for advice and direction.

Chapter 18

Basic Principles of Conflict Resolution and Restoration

As there are many potential causes and manifestations of conflict, so too are there many ways to address and hopefully resolve conflict. Tailor-made conflict assessment and resolution examines the issue/conflict and formulates a strategy that deals specifically with the catalyst and manifestations of the conflict. This is ideally done by all stakeholders involved; however, sometimes stakeholders don't wish to be involved in discussion that may lead to resolution.

Often both individuals (or a group of individuals) in conflict think that they are justified and right and that the other individual or individuals are wrong. These individuals often think resolution to a conflict is biased and have difficulty seeing the other individual's situation, attitude and perspective.

There are several common emotional and cognitive obstacles that can exacerbate conflict. Some of these are conscious deliberation; however, some may be unconscious.

The outside assistance of a mediator is another aspect of conflict resolution. This mediator must be a trained, neutral third party to aid in dispute consensus and resolution. The mediator should not impose a solution but encourage the disputants to examine the reasons behind their positions.

Mediators work with all disputants together and separately to ascertain a complete picture of the dispute, allowing them to discern what is factual and what is based on emotion. It is then that the mediator helps all disputants to discover a resolution that is practical, sustainable, voluntary and nonbinding.

In conflict resolution theory there are two key areas to address and prevent conflict in the education environment.

1. Formal Policies & Procedures

In the modern world, most organisations have conflict resolution policies and procedures in place. This includes education organisations that deal with adult learning. Negative emotions and actions can build from something mild and benign but if left unaddressed can and often will develop into potentially serious workplace matters that impact greatly on relationships and productivity. The sooner conflict is addressed and strategies are put in place, the sooner relationships are re-established or at least managed and the sooner productivity is restored. This is why it is vital for organisations to have in place formalised policies and procedures to address conflict.

In the adult education environment, a disputant may first wish to approach the facilitator/trainer with their concerns. Alternatively, they may go straight to the manager of the training organisation, their own workplace or the governing body that placed them in that training environment. This means there are many different avenues for disputants to take when reporting concerns. If the disputant has an issue or distrust with someone at a certain level, they are not required to report to that same person. This allows internal accountability.

Honest feedback promotion is integral to conflict resolution. Conflict in a learning environment occurs between other learners, facilitators, or the organisation, when courteous but honest feedback is not given, or communication is stifled.

Frustration and conflict can occur when an individual's needs are not met or perhaps their ideas and opinions are not listened to.

If detrimental or negative feedback is given this can also cause a non-productive learning environment. This negative attitude can be contagious in a group environment especially if the concerns are felt by more than one within a group.

It is important for a facilitator and the learning organisation to give honest and timely feedback and by setting the example of putting feedback procedures in place, participants are comfortable and more likely to give honest feedback. Honest constructive feedback instils a sense of trust in all stakeholders.

2. Avoid Making the Problem Personal

When addressing conflict, take the individual and personalities out of the process and focus solely on the issues presented. This will remove the possibility of taking sides or not with an individual. Removing any bias or predetermined ideas regarding the situation. Conflict will often promote a negative and at times antagonistic mindset towards combatants. Focusing solely on the issues helps to bypass that.

Be mindful that individuals tend to view conflict differently. This has to do with their past experiences, their relationships with the conflict stakeholders and their own innate personality and character and how that relates to their own conflict resolutions. This is why it is important to focus on the issue—this removes a right and wrong determination before the conflict has been dealt with.

It's important to start an education workplace conflict resolution procedure by a collaborative problem-solving approach. Never ask those involved closed questions that require only yes or no answers. This is not productive and will not yield information to address the conflict. Ensure that all stakeholders have the time they need to express their point of view, encouraging them not to be emotive but concentrate on relaying facts.

The key attribute in dealing with any conflict resolution situation is for all stakeholders to listen. Listen closely to what is being said. Examine possible deeper agendas or underlying reasons behind the conflict and if through listening you agree with the stakeholders that there are other issues to be addressed then deal with them after the immediate issue is resolved and strategies have been put in place for restoration.

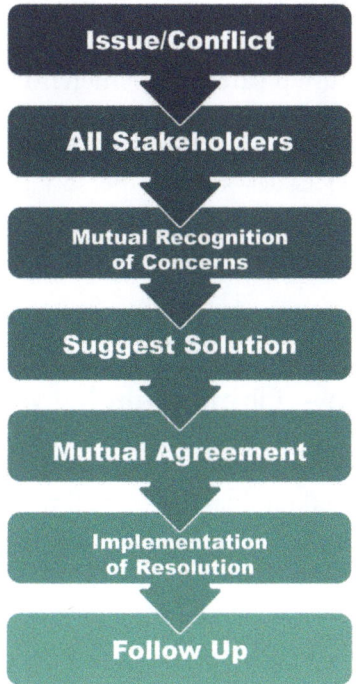

Untenable Situations

If all avenues to resolve or reconcile have been exhausted and all strategies used to modify a participant's adverse behaviour have been followed yet still no change or adequate resolution is attained, then the participant may be asked to leave the education environment.

Discipline or Behavioural Correction

Workplace education or re-education may result as corrective action against an employee for inappropriate or dangerous behaviour or practices.

An example may be if a racist comment is delivered in the workplace. The offender may be instructed as part of discipline procedures to undertake cultural awareness training either online or via internal or external educators.

A non-disciplinary behaviour may be the incorrect use of production equipment by an employee because they were incorrectly instructed on its correct use, so the employee and the original supervising instructor need to learn how to use it safely and efficiently.

Simply put, where there is a discrepancy between two or more individuals over many and varied issues such as personality clashes or need and wants of resources or clash of ideals, opinions and philosophies, there may be conflict.

Early intervention – 'Connection before correction'

Once a conflict has been identified as potentially emerging or has already established between stakeholders, it is vital to address the conflict and the reasons for the conflict as soon as possible. Early intervention is key.

A Created Reality

This is one of the hardest situations to deal with, as it pertains to a participant having formulated in their own version of events, which are very real to the affected participant. They can support their reasoning with examples, even though the intent behind such examples have been skewed or misremembered/misinterpreted.

When this situation arises and organisational procedures have failed or are seen as inadequate, then it is recommended that a third-party mediator or arbitrator is commissioned as an external consultant.

Chapter 19

A Captive Audience

Before You Enter

As part of reformation or transition programs within most corrective services organisations, inmates are offered or mandated the opportunity to attend training courses. This can be a stressful yet rewarding experience for both the participants and the trainer/educator. This type of specialised training is not for every trainer. However, the overall benefits to both incarcerated participants and trainer far outweigh the stress and apprehension you may feel in this environment.

Corrective services institutions ensure the safety of the inmates, staff and any external visitors that have immediate contact with inmates personally or professionally. There are numerous mandatory protocols that are in place to ensure the safety of people in close proximity with inmates. These protocols may vary from one corrective services organisation to another and also with the level of inmate classification.

To enter a corrective services establishment often requires stringent and thorough personal identification and purpose declaration as well as potentially some related short-course training. You will be required to register for digital identification in the form of fingerprint and/or iris scanning, as well as producing some form of personal identification. You will be briefed by corrective services officers regarding the dos and don'ts of their particular centre as well as personal safety protocols.

You may be asked to carry a personal duress alarm that may or may not have a 'tilt' alert as well as a user 'alert' button and/or an internal frequency handheld Citizen Band (CB) radio. These must be worn on a user's belt and in the case of a 'tilt' activated unit, the user must not cause the duress unit to move from the vertical standing or sitting position, as this may 'falsely' activate an alarm at the corrective service 'officers' station. If required, the user can also use the CB radio to alert officers on a pre-determined/designated channel frequency.

Once you are in contact with the inmates there are important things to remember relating to your training room, further personal security requirements and appropriate behaviour and interaction with inmates.

Firstly, ensure that you have obtained all necessary security information relating to the teaching environment, including location of fixed duress alarms. These are generally large red buttons attached to a wall near an exit door. Check where security cameras are positioned as well. Secondly make sure that you know the location of ancillary, non-custodial staff associated with the area you are conducting training in. They should be easily contactable if not present in the training area for the duration of your session. Thirdly, a custodial staff member may also be allocated to your area of operation for the duration of the session. This is often dependent upon the inmate's level of security. For example, low or medium classified inmates may or may not require any custodial or non-custodial staff to be present at all.

Interaction with Inmates

As an educator/facilitator whose students/participants are incarcerated inmates, it is imperative that you present a nonjudgmental attitude towards these participants. Do not enter this training/facilitator environment with preconceived ideas. Do not ask questions about the inmate's life history or why they are now incarcerated. Avoid or close down discussion instigated by the inmate relating to crimes they may have committed and conditions in the gaol.

In most cases, inmates have a lot of time to think and plan, and will try to manipulate outsiders into passing messages on or report conditions, as well as other coercions. These requests must be reported to correctional centre authorities at the earliest opportunity. As an outsider, a facilitator is not allowed to have any interactions with an inmate that may be seen as subversive or contrary to the conditions and regulations governing an incarcerated individual or the correctional facility.

In a lot of cases, the incarcerated individual will feel that they are innocent or wrongly accused of the crimes they have been incarcerated for. Facts may give way to emotive banter as they try and make a sympathetic ally of you as a precursor of them requesting aid from you in some form. This could be asking you to pass on information or bring forbidden contraband into the gaol. This is illegal and may result in the trainer/educator being charged.

Treat the inmate with professional respect. We all make mistakes in life and these people are no different. Treat the inmate in a training/learning environment the same way you would treat any other participant. Having said that, there are still several considerations that need to be made in a correctional facility toward inmates.

Room Agreement

The room agreement is to be mutually drawn up on a whiteboard and agreed to by trainers and inmates prior to course or subject commencement. These are behavioural guidelines for the class or individual that the trainer/educator must adhere to as well throughout the length of delivery.

Involve the inmates in formulating points for the room agreement. Inmates may have been through many training/education programs over their incarcerated time, sop they may freely offer points from previous agreements presented.

No Bad Language

This includes common and colloquial words or terms and localised 'Jail Speak' used as insulting, offensive or degrading language between inmates. Ask an officer to inform you of any words or phrases that you should be aware of.

Show Respect

This is very much a two-way process where the facilitator needs to show respect to the inmates, just as the inmates must show respect towards the facilitator. Maintaining dignity is imperative and the facilitator must always act in a respectful and professional manner towards the inmates.

Avoid Spotlighting

When an individual is continually asked for input or general comment, that individual may feel isolated, picked on or even favoured. This is called spotlighting. If this occurs, that individual or other participants may cease input altogether for fear of being isolated or picked on. Spotlighting can humiliate and embarrass an individual and is to be avoided at all costs. Spotlighting may cause a perceived humiliation to the inmate in front of other participants. This may make it very difficult and uncomfortable for that inmate after the education session when they return to the general prison population. The humiliation incurred by an individual may impact negatively on the already established hierarchical ordering within the general population of the correctional facility.

Don't Interrupt

Allow opportunities for all participants to speak their mind in relevance to the topic and not be cut off by others or the facilitator.

Keep to Time

It is important for the facilitator to have a clear schedule of breaks that must be adhered to. Morning and afternoon tea breaks as well as Lunch must fit into clear, well-defined time boundaries. These breaks must fit into the respective institution's mandatory activities such as muster, 'buy ups', inmates' lunch or laundry duties, and attendance at medical clinics. Depending on the correctional facility, other mandatory inmate duties may occur, and inmates must be allowed to leave the training to perform these duties.

Note: Muster is a series of scheduled or random roll calls of inmates that will happen at various times throughout the day. Unless prearrangement has been made, the inmate will be required to attend muster. 'Buy ups' is where the inmate can purchase items from a canteen type service. These 'buy up' days and times vary from facility to facility but are well sought after by the inmates. If possible, training schedules should be adjusted to align breaks with scheduled 'buy up' sessions.

No War Stories

Inmates will often try and impress, threaten or obtain shock value by telling stories about their criminal activity and how they came to be incarcerated. This is not to be tolerated in a learning environment. At times they will gain satisfaction at observing your reaction to what they are telling you. The best way to counter this is maintain a neutral, non-fazed persona. This nullifies the inmate's intent.

Seating

Depending on the type of training, classroom seating positions are important. For safety and comfort, ensure that no inmates are seated or standing between the session delivery area and the exit area/door. Position seating in a horseshoe configuration, ensuring that there is no individual or small cluster of individuals is sitting in a dominant or subservient seating positions. All participants must be seated in the facilitator's line of sight.

General Information

Inside a correctional facility are several levels of authority that facilitators should be aware of. The custodial staff have ultimate authority over inmates and directional authority over non-custodial staff that are present within the facility. Non-custodial staff facilitate internal and external education programs as well as well as counselling, career advice, transition programs to name a few.

Inmates within the correctional facility are classified (classo), according to the severity and nature of their crime, misdemeanour. For example, three broad classifications could be minimum, medium and maximum security. Within these classifications' inmates will have varying opportunity to interact with other inmates within their respective areas of classification and housing. These are unofficial and generally uncondoned principles of hierarchical ordering. This means there could be leaders and subservients within a group or classification. The hierarchical ordering can be established through several elements that include age, outside status or reputation, toughness, violence or culture. This established order will go through several power shifts in an inmate's time in incarceration and the politics of these groups and position in the ordering needs to be constantly maintained and manipulated for personal gain. All officers frown upon these internal power groups forming and operating; however, they are very hard to identify and control. A lot of these groups are ego-driven, and as a trainer/facilitator it is dangerous to engage with inmates who are involved in this hierarchical subculture within the facility and specifically the learning environment. If this unofficial and uncondoned subculture has a disruptive or aggressive impact within the learning environment, then it is to be reported immediately and entered into the trainer/facilitator's session file notes when appropriate.

Under no circumstances is the facilitator to give comment or opinion on areas outside the scope of the education to be delivered. This is unprofessional and could adversely affect the authority and respect that you as a facilitator/educator have with inmates and officers in attendance.

Above all, when training within a corrective services facility, adhere to every regulation and directive given by that facility's governing officers.

Training within a corrective services organisation can be a very rewarding experience in many ways. You as a facilitator, are never to ask why the inmate is in jail or how long will they be in jail or enter into any personal discussion with them or divulge personal information about yourself or others. You must always take and except the inmate on face value and determine a professional relationship and training strategy based on your own observations and interactions with the inmate. Put aside any predetermined judgements on how and why the individual became incarcerated and any unsociable behaviour in jail and treat the inmate as you would any other participant on the outside.

Some inmates may be incarcerated for extended periods of time. In that time, their only interactions are with fellow inmates or custodial and non-custodial officers and occasional visitors. Boredom is a common condition with most inmates and to relieve institutional induced melancholy, the inmates may construct ways to relieve it. Sometimes this may be in the form of innocuous, benign banter and practical jokes. It can also take the form of manipulative and cunning words and actions aimed at eliciting a response that gives the inmate a form of personal satisfaction. While most things in their lives have been taken away or controlled through their incarceration, they are still able to have input into the lives of others through their responses and action. This is often a negative interaction and is strictly forbidden by correctional facilities and training organisations. If the trainer/facilitator feels they are being drawn into negative manipulation, they are not to react or respond but report the incident as soon as feasible to correction facility officers and record such incidents in the training organisation's session file notes.

In many cases the inmates must attend training because it is a mandated part of their incarceration conditions. They also may be in attendance as part of a court arrangement to pay off state or Commonwealth debt such as parking or speeding fines. Then there are those who attend because they want to be there and realise how they will personally benefit by attending self-development courses. No matter what the motive is for attending, an equipped educator can inspire and inform an inmate by sharing knowledge and understanding. The inmate that absorbs this knowledge can experience life-changing impacts relating to goals, purpose and life direction. These occurrences are light bulb moments that encourage both the inmate and the trainer/facilitator, and can be extremely satisfying for the trainer to observe. The inmate is appreciative of someone sharing knowledge and understanding and may profess to make life changes because of what they have learnt. This is why training/facilitating in a corrective services facility can be a most rewarding experience for all stakeholders.

Chapter 20

Verbal Punctuation

'Verbally Punctuate your delivery to create better meaning to the structure and form of your delivery.'

David W. Mayne

A presenter can use various elements of their voice to produce desired punctuation, intonation, emphasis or topic change.

As in nonverbal communication, there is a baseline of normal verbal presentation, and a presenter can use variations to that baseline as an effective presentation tool. These variations may include the rise or fall of volume or variation of tone or changes of inflection and speed however, more often the most effective use of verbal punctuation is a strategic combination of all elements mentioned.

Volume

The rise and fall in presentation volume by a presenter are primary tools to emphasise a point or soften a poignant topic. If there is an important/vital area being covered in a presentation, then a slight rise in volume, distinct from the presenter's normal baseline reference, will drive the point ensuring that participants take greater notice at that time. If the presenter wishes to present a more reflective or poignant topic then they might wish to speak in a softer, lower volume. This sets the mood for the participants by the presenter, matching the topic being presented. This is brought about through two primary ways. Firstly, the contrast in presenter's delivery and secondly, the loudness may bring participants back to focus as a verbal alert mechanism.

Tone

Tone often refers to sound, as in music or song. However, when referred to in speech or voice, it refers to sound or feeling conveyed by the way someone speaks. For example, 'His tone of voice was serious, and I felt I was in trouble.' Tone in verbal presentation can distinguish shades of meaning that may reveal greater intent of the presenter. It can set or change the mood of an education environment simply through the tone of delivery. A tone is a kind of sound you hear in a person's voice that triggers emotional responses in the listener. An educator can predetermine the tone they wish to set for participants in a learning environment. All the factors discussed in this chapter contribute towards the tone of a presentation.

Pace of Speech

Pace of speech in any education delivery scenario is much maligned but highly important in communicating an accurate message to participants. It can mean the difference between full understanding and knowledge recall, and little or no understanding leading to ignorance, disinterest and potential assessment/course non-competency.

The speed at which we speak is our pace of speech. It's usually expressed in words per minute (WPM). In conversational speech an individual can speak as quickly as 180-200 WPM, with over 200 WPM too fast when presenting information needed in an educational environment. A facilitator/trainer should aim to speak at a maximum of 120-150 WPM.

There are several important factors that can influence a facilitator's pace of speech. This may include nervousness due to unfamiliarity with the topic to be delivered or unfamiliarity with the participants or the innate speaking pace of the individual presenting. They may already be fast talkers and may need to consciously make an effort to monitor and modify the pace at which they speak in a delivery session. Other presenters may quicken their pace if they are excited or passionate about a topic. Self-awareness and self-adjustment are the optimum method of pace regulation.

This also goes for the presenter whose pace of speech is very slow. This also may be caused by factors such as fear of delivering the wrong information or hoping for a more dramatic or poignant delivery style. The presenter delivers in a more deliberate or cautious pace that may give participants a feeling or unease, possibly assuming that the presenter is not sure of information they a relaying or that the presenter is wishing for the participants to interject by deliberately inserting pauses for the participants to ask questions.

A slower speaking style may be implemented if the general dynamics of the participants require a slower paced delivery to assure greater understanding and recall. This may be due to cognitive or intellectual limitations of individuals or a group of participants.

In combination with other elements listed in this chapter, pace of speaking can be an effective tool of delivery for any presenter.

Inflection

Is used in speech to express a grammatical function. This is achieved through the use of 'peaks' and 'troughs'. For example, when a presenter is attempting to ask a question, their tone or pitch will rise slightly at the end of a sentence. If the presenter wishes to end a sentence or finish a topic, their tone or pitch will lower slightly. This essentially is verbal punctuation. This helps create the contrast effect. Volume also plays a part in verbal punctuation and inflection. Volume can demonstrate an important or poignant topic or sentence or be used to regain the attention of participants through use of the 'contrast effect'.

The contrast effect is a pronounced or sometimes subtle variation in verbal or nonverbal presentation. For example, you may wish to give an important part of your presentation more emphasis. If you raise or lower your voice in direct contrast to the volume of the rest of your presentation, this can grab the conscious and subconscious attention of participants. This can also be achieved by a variation in pitch and tone and complimented by a variation in nonverbal presentation as well, such as hand, arm, head and other nonverbal presentations.

After a time, familiarity would have established both a verbal and nonverbal baseline of normal presentation behaviour. This variation from this baseline of normal presentation is deemed the contrast effect.

Conversational Oscillation

Conversational oscillation is how we present our conversation in a relaxed and familiar environment. For example, when two old friends are talking to each other, there is a random rise and fall in their vocal oscillation. There isn't a set pattern governed by variation due to emphasis or stringent verbal punctuation.

Minimal conversational oscillation is a small or minimal use of verbal inflection. The presenter speaks in a monotone way with little variation to tone, volume or pitch. Other than for comedic purposes, this type of presentation should not be used in educational delivery. Facilitators delivering in this baseline style will have great difficulty in maintaining the attention and interest of the participants they are presenting possibly lose the respect of some participants.

'Peaks' and 'troughs' in vocal oscillation is often heard by inexperienced TV or radio presenters or educational presenters who have not gained confidence or knowledge in what they hope to present and in their own ability to present. There is little or no conversational oscillation with these presenters. Nerves or unfamiliarity with the topic to be presented will cause the presenter to end each sentence with upward 'peak' inflection. This gives the impression to the listener that the presenter is nervous or not sure of the information they are providing or that they are telling an untruth to the participants. This peaking and troughing gives no regularity to verbal punctuation in delivery and to the listener can be heard as disjointed, confusing and annoying.

Modulation

In speech, modulation is when the presenter can adjust or control how something is being said. For example, the presenter may lower their voice and emphasise a loud whisper. This makes what the presenter is saying more poignant or dramatic. This way of transferring important information may stay in the participant's mind and be able to be recalled from memory a lot easier because of the facilitator's method of verbal delivery. A change in modulation always involves a deliberate modification or even a slight variation in pitch or volume of the presenter. This variation can be adjusted as per presenter's verbal requirements and desired impact.

Linguistics

Because of the potential variation in the nationality, culture and primary languages of participants, it is important to understand the basics of linguistic science.

Linguistics is the research of language. It analyses language form, meaning, and context, as well as analysing social, cultural, historical and political elements that influence language. Those who research linguistics traditionally study human language by observing the relationship between sound and meaning. Meaning is studied through directly spoken or written form through the discipline of semantics, as well as in its indirect form through nonverbal gestures under the area of pragmatics. Every element of speech is called a phoneme. How these are organised to cover meaning depends on various linguistic patterns and structures that linguists describe and analyse. It is worth a facilitator or education program formulator to further study the principles of linguistics and their application in the learning environment.

Chapter 21

Cognitive Thought vs Intellectual Thought

'Intelligence can be defined as the ability to obtain knowledge in an adaptive situation, while cognition means general awareness and the ability to gain knowledge in particular ... For example, someone with an exceedingly high IQ may have severe cognitive impairment.'

David W. Mayne

As a presenter/trainer, your perceptions of participants build up with time and experience. The ability to perceive a participant upon observation and interaction can be distorted, however, it is important to discern what is cognitive thought and intellectual thought. It is also important for a presenter to ascertain and act on any cognitive or intellectual hindrances that a learner may be experiencing and, as a presenter/facilitator equipped with that understanding, be able to consider potential variations in presentation of information provided to enable greater understanding and information retention.

In simple terms, intellectual intelligence may be defined as the ability to obtain and use knowledge in an adaptive situation, while cognition means awareness in general, particularly in regard to the ability to learn.

Cognitive disabilities can be disadvantages to learning. A person with this type of problem can experience difficulty in perceiving, recognising, choosing and understanding. It can be an inability to focus for any significant period of time. It may be a problem processing printed text or defective short-term memory. It could be problems with visualising quantities, shapes or designs. It is like a roadblock in the way of the learner's progress.

Someone may have an extremely high IQ yet may have a severe cognitive disability. Numeracy may not be a problem for this person, such in the case of some forms of autism or attention order deficit disorder. However, they can be unable to adequately function when faced with the vocational learning environment due to types of dyslexic manifestations such as the reversing of letters and not being able to process written language. Concentration when talking can also prove to be difficult for these individuals.

A change in delivery method or assessment styles may help compensate for this individual's cognitive limitations. The trainer/assessor should have a good understanding of the individual's cognitive impairment and find alternative methods of learning and assessing for that individual. For example, if the participant has difficulty reading the questions in a written assessment, arrange for that participant hear the questions and respond verbally. Dignity is restored and necessary assessment results acquired.

Intellectual disabilities are specific cognitive difficulties that create a low IQ score and significant problems in the ways learners adapt to new and varying situations. This includes their ability to socialise with others in a learning environment, retain information or take an exam. It is harder for them to understand and apply new information that comes their way.

Once a trainer/assessor determines the nature and severity of the intellectual disability, the trainer is better equipped to design and implement a suitable training/assessing regime for that individual.

Useful strategies for training someone with an intellectual disability can include the following points:

- Present one element at a time to promote sequencing and memorisation.

- Deliver one concept or activity at a time.
- Give several opportunities to practice skills and present knowledge in a number of different learning environments.
- Deliver sessions one-on-one or, if possible, in small groups.
- Consider using both verbal or physical prompting to guide required responses and provide specific verbal praise to reinforce these responses.

It is sometimes much more difficult to accommodate for someone with an intellectual disability than someone with other forms of cognitive impairment. A fundamental deficiency in a person's ability to understand may impact greatly in their ability to participate in a training/assessing environment and may impact on the learning and assessing experience of fellow participants through unintended distraction.

It is beneficial to use tangible materials as a component in effective instruction of participants with intellectual disabilities. Hands-on demonstration and repetition of content by the participant is an effective method of learning with participants with intellectual disabilities. Sometimes this method of delivery and use of low-tech tools can serve to both motivate and empower the participant into effectively completing assessment tasks and working towards completion of required course elements.

Chapter 22

Profiling in the Educational Environment

Who hasn't sat in a coffee shop, bar or bus stop and idly watched the world go by? Benignly watched individuals as they go about their daily lives, interacting with each other.

This observing behaviour is part of human nature. It is an innately curious behaviour for humans to observe others to ascertain possible intention or impact on us and then respond as and if required. This appears to be a primitive behaviour that may have developed out of the need for survival or reproduction purposes. An inquisitive nature with a practical and sometimes crucial purpose. As we humans possess inquiring minds as part of our very being, it is important that we satisfy that curiosity with questions and exploration of thoughts and deeds.

Over many generations the ability to observe, interpret and respond appropriately to what is observed has decreased significantly. This may be due to modes of communication such as television, social media and mobile phones causing less face-to-face communication while increasing non-personal interactions between individuals and groups. Human interactions have been diluted through social media. The ability to effectively read and understand behaviour has been minimised over.

One person observing someone else and making a determination of intent of that individual is effectively profiling the individual being observed. This is not necessarily an invasive or confrontational activity, as it goes on every day either consciously or subconsciously. In the corporate world, profiling at different levels is becoming common. For example, what an individual says during a job interview is no longer the sole consideration for consideration. but heed is taken as to what is not said but seen from a job candidate. Presentation and what is written by candidates in tools such as psychometric analysis surveys and becoming increasingly more relevant.

It is true that some individuals are more intuitive and discerning than others. They are more able to observe another individual and make innate determinations of discernible intent. Others may have difficulty with the same observation and determination process. Their profiling process may be one that requires training and practice, while with others a template or assisting tools already exist. These tools may aid them in the profiling process. These may already be part of their persona and are tools already called upon and well utilised by the observer. Some individuals that fall into the area of being on the 'spectrum' may have an inability to observe and understand subtle or even obvious facial expressions, as well as spoken word that includes paralanguage fluctuations.

Tools that an individual on the spectrum may be able to utilise to help with observation include a pictographic series of facial expressions matched with a description of that possibly emotional expression.

Profiling is at times an inaccurate process, as it can easily be distorted and misinterpretations may occur through the process of observation, listening and determination. There may be both external and internal factors that can cause this distortion, such as mood or general state of being of the observer and the observed at that particular time. External factors may be environmental or noise interference. For example, in an education environment, an observer may see a participant with their head looking down, their arms folded tightly in front of themselves with legs closed together or crossed. This can mean that they are not interested in what is being delivered and they are closed off to the presenter and their message. Alternately, the participant may be just cold or unwell, perhaps finding that they are uncomfortable in their seating position. Profiling in an educational environment is not an exact science, as you are not only dealing with the idiosyncrasies of human nature but the many internal and external variables that can present false truths in observation.

Qualify and Quantify?

Why bother qualifying and quantifying the profiling process for a training education environment? The ability to observe, hear and determine the words and actions of a participant in a learning environment may be a crucial tool for better understanding the dynamics of an individual participant or even a group of participants. Once familiarity with an individual or group is gained, you should have established a baseline of normal behaviour relating to individuals or groups. This is where behavioural assessment (profiling) may be a vital tool to any presenter. A presenter may observe apathetic or disgruntled behaviour expressed by one or more participants and can deal with it through verbal interview with the participant/s to establish a cause for their behaviour and adjust accordingly.

It is important to remember that profiling is not a scientific tool of observation, but is the process of obtaining a holistic overview from a learning environment, current academic situation, or any previous events that may cause a distinct variation from the baseline of normal behaviour. It can provide a guideline as a basis for proactive and effective action by the presenter to rectify or avert possible issues that may have negative consequences on a participant's learning experience.

Examples of What to Look For

Fidgeting – This may indicate that the participant is uncomfortable in their seat or general environment. They may wish to be somewhere else and they are distracted by this. Their thoughts are elsewhere. If this fidgeting movement is part of their baseline of normal behaviour, then these physical manifestations are probably congenital and possibly involuntary and therefore of little consequence in relation to problematic causes.

Privately the participant should be asked about their wellbeing and if there was anything that the facilitator or education provider can do to address any concerns or issues disclosed.

Wide open eyes that flicker left to right and eyelid 'blinking' has increased and perhaps sudden but small head movement and erratic eye movements – This may mean that the participant is nervous, agitated, angry or feeling that they are well out of their comfort zone. This type of body language is common for first day participants or those appointed to undertake training rather than voluntarily present. This may settle over time within the learning environment. If it does not or has just manifested randomly during the course of training, it can be determined that this is a defection from the baseline of normal behaviour is therefore an individual event caused by unidentified factors.

Privately the participant should be asked about their wellbeing and if there was anything that the facilitator or education provider can do to address any concerns or issues disclosed.

Wide open eyes combined high pitched and accelerated speech – This may mean that the participant is very nervous about what they are hearing from you or saying to you. They may either be unsure of the information exchange during a conversation, or they are possibly lying to you. At times this body language is completely benign and is a situational expression of nerves and uneasiness, with little or no negative connotation. That is why it must continually be reiterated that the reading of body language is not a fail-safe method of determining the intent or agenda of an individual.

If any of these behaviours stand out to the facilitator, the participant should be privately asked about their wellbeing and if there is anything that the facilitator or education provider can do to address any concerns or issues disclosed.

Late comers and early goers – There are several possible interpretations relating to participants that habitually arrive for training late or leave early. For the presenter, this is only an issue if it is consistently happening by the participants over a regular period of time. There may be genuine reasons for an individual's apparent tardiness such as transport issues or medical appointments. If the same excuse is used consistently by an individual and the participant is absent so often that it is impacting on their learning outcomes, then a conversation between presenter and participant should take place to explain the current situation from the education provider's position. Suggestions for possible solutions to the participant's tardiness issues should be discussed.

If it is an unavoidable situation for the participant, then options from the presenter/facilitator should be given to the participant with the aim of helping them achieve alternate methods of acquiring information, allowing them to achieve all required educational/training outcomes. If the participant continues to be late for educational sessions and/or leaves sessions early even after the importance of attendance or engagement is given, then the facilitator or other authority from the education provider should query if this area of education is appropriate for the participant at this time.

Holistic Observation

When one individual is observing another individual or group of individuals in a learning, training or interview environment, it is crucial that the observer does not solely accept the immediate expressions given by the individual being observed. It is common and quite possible that the words, paralanguage, actions and micro expressions used may have a base meaning and cause, completely different to the observer's interpretation. To enhance accurate determination, it is prudent for the observer to consider the unseen as well as that which is obvious presented.

What has happened in the participant's life preceding the expressions that the facilitator is observing? These are influences that no one can know apart from the participant. These influencing elements may include possible health issues, or the participant may have something else on their mind that is causing distraction from proactive participation in the learning environment. that is expressed in verbal and nonverbal ways seen by the observer facilitator as a variation to that participants 'Baseline of Normal Behaviour' (BNB). Over time it is always best for an observer to use BNB (Baseline Normal Behaviour) to ascertain consistent variables and therefore a need for concern and potential intervention to help the participant any way that the facilitator can.

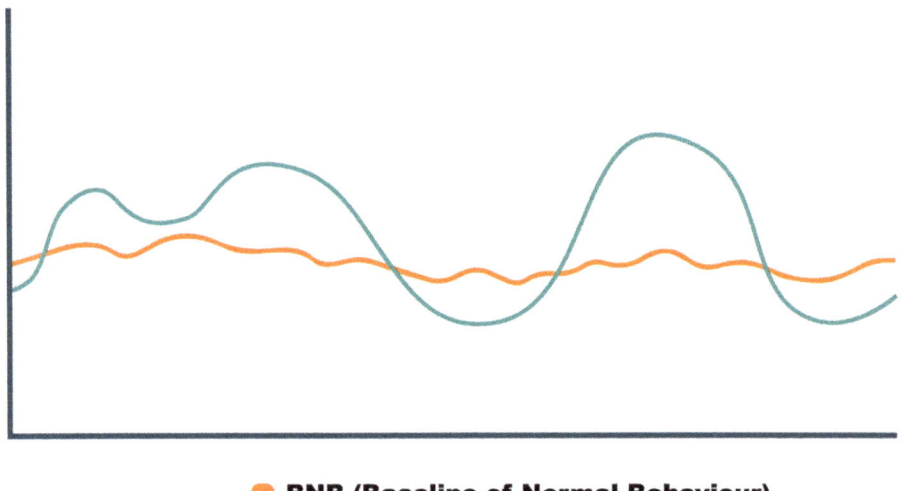

🟠 **BNB (Baseline of Normal Behaviour)**
🟢 **Diversion from BNB**

In summary, the ability to observe others and make a determination about what is heard and seen is an important tool when identifying potential or already established issues of participants within the education/training environment. Early intervention is the key to rectifying any issues that may impact upon a participant's learning experience. Judgements through determination may or may not be accurate. Be prepared for your determination to be incorrect. The more you practice, the more accurate you should become in matching your observations with what is actually and accurately happening within your field of observation. Basically, the more you practice the more discerning you become.

Chapter 23

Audio-Visual Technology

Audio-visual education or multimedia-based education (MBE) is an education tool where attention is given to the audio and visual presentation of the material with the aim of improving understanding, retention and recall.

A Brief History

Educational aids such as audio-visual technology are not new to education. In the 17th century, John Amos Comenius (1592-1670), used pictures as aids to teach. During World War II, audio-visual aids were used by armed forces to plan defence and offence strategies, as well as in personnel training (Encyclopedia Britannica, n.d.).

Audio-visual aids have evolved over many years, from cave paintings and crude pictographs to highly advanced holographic imaging and virtual reality programs. The objective of audio-visual aids is to enhance the facilitator's ability to present education in a simple, effective and easy-to-understand medium for the participants. Audio-visual material makes education more effective as it exposes the participants to many senses. Visual instruction makes vague, abstract ideas more real and understandable to the learners, helping participants understand important elements of course material. There are many positive results for participants who use audio-visual material in a learning environment compared with those who don't.

Objectives of the Use of Audio-Visual (AV) Technology

- To strengthen presenters' skills in making teaching-learning process more effective.
- To attract and retain participant attention.
- To generate interest across different levels of participants.
- To develop session plans that are simple and easy to follow.
- To make the learning process more interactive and interesting.
- To focus on a participant centred approach.

Advantages

In the modern world we use digital tools to improve the teaching-learning process. The use of audio-visual aids allows the participant to remember concepts for longer periods of time. The images convey the same meaning as words, but allow for greater clarity of concept through visualisation, thus bringing effectiveness to the learning process.

Note: One of most common tools we use in classroom are PowerPoint slides, which makes the class more interesting, dynamic and effective. However, even this medium of AV delivery is quickly becoming outdated. PowerPoint presentations that are overdone can be distracting and highly unnecessary.

Sometimes a presenter will use PowerPoint presentations with graphics, unnecessary backgrounds and over the top slide changes. This is commonly referred to as 'Death By PowerPoint'. This is not conducive to a smooth and consistent presentation. It will actually distract the participant from what is being presented by the facilitator. The simple and concise formular for designing a PowerPoint presentation are the three B's.

Be brief→Be bright→Be gone

This means only display the slides that demonstrate an area or topic that is to be presented and discussed. Be positive and visually stimulating but not over the top. Ensure brevity through the number of slides and the content they hold.

Integrating technology into an education environment helps participants to experience things virtually.

For example, if the presenter wants to give a session on leadership, it is possible for the presenter to show photos of well-known political or corporate leaders or even show a clip of a famous leader's speech. These AV presentations complement and enhance the leadership topic being presented affirming what needs to be presented through relevant and appealing examples.

The use of audio-visual aids helps maintain attention in the learning environment, since all the participants' attention is focused on learning. Interactive sessions also develop critical thinking and questioning. These are crucial components of the facilitation-learning process.

Audio-visual technology provides opportunities for effective communication between facilitators and participants. For example, English as a Foreign Language students may have a lack of understanding of what is being said and therefore decreased motivation. Such difficulties can be overcome by auditory tools as purpose of communication and visual tools for more exposure to the educational content being provided.

Students learn when they are motivated and curious about something. Traditional verbal instructions can be boring for some students.

However, use of audio-visual technology provides motivation to students by piquing their curiosity and stimulating their interests in the subjects through variation in delivery.

Virtual & Augmented Reality (VR & AR)

Virtual reality (VR) is not a recent development. However, since the COVID-19 pandemic, virtual reality has become more widely used and developed in many fields, including medicine and education.

Virtual Reality (VR) is considered an Audio Visual (AV) tool in education. It is a simulated experience that uses pose tracking and 3D near-eye displays (goggles/eye pieces) to give the user an immersive and almost first-person experience of a virtual world. Applications of virtual reality include entertainment (particularly video games), education (such as medical or military training) and business (such as virtual meetings).

At the time of writing, standard virtual reality systems use either virtual reality headsets or multi-projected environments (VR Rooms) to generate realistic images, sounds and other sensory simulants that give a user a physical presence in a virtual environment. A person using virtual reality equipment can look around the artificial world, they can move in it, and possibly interact with virtual features, items or even people.

The effect is commonly created by VR headsets consisting of a head-mounted display with a small screen directly in front of the eyes but can also be created through specially designed rooms with multiple large screens.

Virtual reality typically incorporates auditory and video feedback. It may also allow other types of sensory feedback through haptic technology. Haptic technology 'creates a physical feeling such as a push or vibration so that you know, for example, when you have pressed or touched something on a screen' (Cambridge Dictionary, 2024).

In adult/vocational education, virtual and augmented reality (VR/AR are increasingly being used to engage students in a greater and more interactive and immersive manner. By creating virtual environments that replicate real-life scenarios, educators can provide students with immersive learning experiences and inspire their engagement and creativity. VR/AR can also aid students struggling with traditional education methods and motivate them to explore new academic or vocational interests. VR/AR can be used at all education levels, from preschool to vocational and tertiary education. As the technology continues to advance, it can be expected to see more use and innovations in the area of VR.

Disadvantages

Too much audio-visual material used at one time can result in boredom and distractions. It is useful only if it is implemented effectively. Considering that each learning situation varies, it is important to know that not all concepts can be learned effectively through audio-visual materials.

Equipment like projectors, speakers and headphones are often costly, hence some learning providers cannot afford it. It may take time for a presenter to prepare sessions to have an AV component. Time may also be lost in gaining familiarity with new equipment. Some participants may feel reluctant to ask questions while AV is being utilised.

Unless participants are instructed to write questions down during an AV presentation, productive discussion may be lost. In places where electricity is not available i.e. in rural areas, it is not feasible to use audio-visual aids that requires electricity unless a portable generator is being implemented. This may cause other problems such as noise and operational maintenance.

Audio visual aids are important tools for the teaching learning process. It helps the teacher to present the lesson effectively and students learn and retain the concepts better and for longer duration. Use of audio-visual aids improves students' critical and analytical thinking. It helps to remove abstract concepts through visual presentation.

However, improper and unplanned use of these aids can have negative effect on the learning outcome. Therefore, educators should be well trained through in-service training to maximize the benefits of using these aids. The syllabus should be designed such that there are options to activity-based learning through audio-visual aids.

Equipment

Equipment commonly used for audio-visual presentations may include:

- Televisions
- LCD projectors
- Film projectors
- Slide projectors
- Opaque projectors (episcopes and epidiascopes)
- Overhead projectors

These audio-visual aids must be used to enhance a subject/topic delivery and should never be used to dominate or replace a presentation. The use of too many audio-visual tools at one time or in close succession will only serve to bombard the participants with too much information and unnecessary stimuli that may distract them from the facilitator's desired outcomes.

All audio-visual resources must be relevant to the topic delivered, must support the information being relayed by the facilitator and must not confuse or distort the information given.

In summary, audio-visual aids are important tools for the teaching-learning process. It helps the teacher to present the lesson effectively and students learn and retain the concepts better and for longer duration. Use of audio-visual aids improves students' critical and analytical thinking. It helps to remove abstract concepts through visual presentation. However, improper and unplanned use of these aids can have negative effect on the learning outcome. Therefore, educators should be well trained through in-service training to maximize the benefits of using these aids. The syllabus should be designed such that there are options to activity-based learning through audio-visual aids.

Chapter 24

Video Conferencing Platforms

In 2020 the world changed. A global pandemic emerged that had radical and permanent impact on the world as we have known it. The impact has had substantial influence on almost every facet of life. Our interpersonal skills have had to evolve and adapt to suit many catalysts such as government and organisational policies, procedures and legislations.

The pandemic had a great influence on our personal and professional lives. How we now conduct our way of life has changed. Some of these changes have been enduring, despite the fact we have largely returned to a pre-pandemic way of life again.

Communication has undergone substantial development since the COVID-19 pandemic, especially in the education and training space. One of the largest developments is the proliferation and normalisation of audio-visual conferencing tools in classrooms.

Audio-visual conferencing tools first came into prominence when they were first put on display at the New York World's Fair in 1968 as a glimpse of a 'space age' future. Today there are many commercial video conferencing platforms.

What Program to Use?

This depends on various factors that may include what you are trying to present, where you wish to present it and who you wish to present to. Who are your participants and what information is it that you hope to deliver? These questions are key to deciding the online conferencing program you wish to use.

Identify what other requirements will be, such as the size of your group. Do you need breakout rooms and sessions? Do you require closed or open questioning? What part do chat room questions and answers play in the education session? Will you as facilitator be answering participants questions during the session or will the questions accumulate until the end? This may determine the program you use and to what level and cost you subscribe to. Common software used in the educational environment include, Skype, Zoom, Microsoft Teams, and Webex Meetings. There are others but for ease and access for both presenter and participants these are more than adequate.

Booking Sessions

When booking a session on any online conferencing program or app, ensure that you are fully aware of the format and conditions of that program and how it may impinge on a facilitator's presentation. It is important for a facilitator to carefully examine all suitable and relevant attributes of a commercial online conferencing program to determine the best vehicle for delivery for both presenters and participants.

Who is your Audience?

When considering what online conferencing platform to use for education/instruction purposes, those delivering must primarily consider who the participants are. Where are they from and what is their ease of access to the internet and the online platforms for consistent and reliable participation during a session?

All issues or potential problems with the platform and the structure of delivery and how this impinges on the participants and the facilitator should be discussed and clarified well in advance of a delivery session. All stakeholders should be made aware of what is required when participating on a online conferencing platform.

Venue Dynamics: Lighting and Sound

As all online conferencing platforms are different, it is important for an education body and the facilitators that are presenting to be fully aware of the nuances that individualise a platform. Facilitators must make suitable adjustments to delivery and setting to accommodate those differences with the aim of presenting the easiest, reliable and most efficient platform to enhance participant and facilitator experience.

Important elements to consider are sound and lighting. This of course is primarily the participants' responsibility. However, it is ideal that a set of simple standards for participation is laid out long before a session is commenced.

The face of both the facilitator and participants should be well illuminated. A front-on soft light is preferable instead of above, below or side lighting, as this will cast shadows on the face and limit interpretation of facial expressions for both facilitator and participants. It is imperative that the facilitator has excellent lighting as it is the facilitator that participants are looking to for direction. A clear view of all participants' faces does not only aid in the transfer of information in any education session, but it is also a polite substitute for a face-to-face presentation.

Check the lighting of the room that you are broadcasting from. Ensure through a pre-test that the light is adequate and consistent. Do this also for sound. Check your sound levels through the platform's pre-broadcast settings. Pick a suitable level, no more than two-thirds of the provided scale. This may adjust once a facilitator has done a sound check with participants just prior to the delivery session.

Participants should be encouraged to set the same sound level. A pre-sound and lighting check should be done by every participating individual prior to log-in and session commencement. A final online check must also be done. However, if every participant has done their personal sound and lighting checks then the online check should take no more than three minutes prior to session commencement.

Breakout or Waiting Room

Waiting rooms and breakout rooms are an important tool in some online educational delivery sessions. These can be used prior to commencement. This gives uniform participant entry into the main facilitator-led delivery session, leaving the facilitator opportunity for final preparation and online arrangements if required. The facilitator must have full control of entry from the participant waiting room. It is imperative that the facilitator/coordinator of the online conferencing session logs on at the nominated time. This is not only courteous but also professional and enhances the reputations of the facilitator and the RTO.

Online breakout rooms are used to replace face-to-face small group discussions. These are opportunities for the facilitator to separate individuals into virtual discussion or workshop groups that can discuss and provide ideas and opinions in a smaller group that, at the designated time, will re-join the main group. All participants will then discuss what was determined in the breakout sessions.

It is important in these breakout sessions that the facilitator or the group themselves designate a spokesperson for that group. This alleviates the possibility of everyone speaking during the group summation period. It is also important that before the breakout session begins, each group is made fully aware by the facilitator of the scope of topic to be discussed and the timeframe allocated to the breakout spokesperson for summation of the discussion.

Screen Sharing

Screen sharing pages are dependent upon relevance to the session and the topic delivered. A participant's wish to share their screen must be discussed with the facilitator or invited by the facilitator before the commencement of the online session. The participant's presentation must have content and sharing time limitations. The content should be agreed upon by the facilitator and the time restraints mandatory for all screen sharers. The shared content must be uncomplicated with only relevant and poignant details that either express the required information or opinion of the presenting participant or the content required for the session or course by the facilitator. The participant who is sharing information must also speak to what is being presented and be cautioned not to drift off topic. The facilitator, as online chair of the session, must freely adjudicate any variations to the agreed and forewarned session protocols.

Other Considerations

Due to the lack of the many benefits of a face-to-face presentation, the facilitator must take into consideration the limitations presented and adjust the session preparation and delivery accordingly.

A facilitator delivering through an online platform must be conscientious of slowing down their speech and limiting micro expressions and other macro body language. On a limited computer screen, these subtle body languages may be open for misinterpretation and therefore distort intent and meaning to what's being relayed by the facilitator.

Despite being an online scenario, it is still important to dress appropriately for the session. A facilitator must wear the same clothes as they would during a face-to-face session. Participants are encouraged to do the same. This gives professional credibility to the facilitator and the RTO. Unsuitable attire may be seen as devaluing the course or session by participants and may reflect badly on the RTO. This may transpose onto the participants as a negative or apathetic attitude that could be reflected in a participant's attitude to the course/session in the form of tardiness, or even impacted completion results.

Avoid colours and shades that are too bright or too dull. This may distract participants as you as facilitator will be the centre of their field of view for the majority of the session. Therefore, it is important to wear the clothes you would normally wear in a face-to-face session. This includes full cover. Many embarrassing online video conferencing incidents have occurred because session participants, including the facilitator, traded professionalism for comfort and exposed a personal area that was not or only partially covered. For example, I witnessed a presenter stand up and the camera displayed the facilitator's undergarments from the waist down. Negligence caused an extremely embarrassing situation to this group of management and leadership participants, and shortly after, embarrassment to the facilitator once he was made aware of his oversight.

Emoticons

The use of emoticons is an important tool of nonverbal communication during an online conferencing session. Different online platforms have different emoticons and different access and use procedures. The relevant emoticon protocols should be explained for each delivery session and the facilitator should ensure that all participants follow those protocols. For example, some sessions may require in-session questions or comments to be stated. Participants will have access to a 'raise hand' emoticon if they wish to ask a question. Facilitators should have access to all available emoticons. However, they should only use the ones that are relevant to the session. The use of certain emoticons should be declared to the participants before the commencement of the session or at the pre-commencement briefing session or email.

Chat question by the participants may be asked during the session but may not be addressed by the facilitator until the nominated question time at the end of the session. The structure of some online sessions may require that all participants need to continually input chat messages as part on online general discussion. Other emoticons may be used at the discretion of the facilitator. For example, there may be an emoticon that the participants are able to use to notify the facilitator of urgent questions, statements or issues. The underlying emoticon protocol is that the Facilitator or RTO determine what and when emoticons should be used.

Microphone and Camera Etiquette

A major tool is the camera and microphone on/off switch. This can be one of the most important attributes of an online conferencing session and protocols must be well adhered to by the facilitator and participants.

The session or course structure dictates at what time and for how long the microphone of participants should be switched off and then back on. Participants can also ask to speak via a pre-determined emoticon or other signal to the facilitator. Microphone levels should have already been adjusted and set by the facilitator and the participants at the pre-session microphone checks. It is expected that during any facilitator's presentation, all participants are muted. This avoids interruptions and the flow of the presentation; however, all participants must be made aware that this is not a negative and controlling blocking of participants but an overall courteous act to stop interruptions and distraction by others during the facilitator's delivery.

Camera etiquette is important as over the last few years of increased use of videoing conferencing, formal and informal protocols for online camera use have developed and in some cases instigated and even mandated.

In a delivery session, all participants, including the facilitator, must be visible to all. There are extenuating circumstances that can determine when and for how long an individual's camera is switched off. If a participant or facilitator needs to switch off their camera for a period of time during a delivery session or during a nominated question time, then it must be pre-arranged and declared. This is a courtesy to all participants. If the same thing happened in a face-to-face situation in adult learning, a participant would ask the facilitator for a leave of absence for a short period of time. The luxury of face-to-face interaction is not possible in an online video conferencing situation, therefore notification or even permission sought to take visible leave is not only courteous to all participants but also seen as professional. This should be as brief as possible as it may impinge on the participants learning experience or group dynamics if that participant is part of an online team.

If the session is to be recorded by the facilitator, as a courtesy and in some cases a requirement. All participants should be consulted regarding the recording of all or part of the session and asked if they are happy with the recording taking place. On most online conferencing platforms, an automatically generated screen notification informs all participants that the session is or about to be recorded. At the pre-session briefing, all participants must be made aware that the session or part of the session will be recorded. If a participant has a reason that they do not wish to be recorded, it is at that time or in speaking to the facilitator privately that an arrangement can be made. This may include having the camera off for that participant. However, this is only in extenuating and justified circumstances.

The frequency of video conferencing use in education has exponentially increased since the COVID-19 pandemic that coincided with advancement in technical communication. New etiquette protocols are being developed for not only the facilitator but also the participants. There are some basics that have not been covered in this chapter earlier, such as what not to do while on a video conferencing session. A participant or facilitator should not mute then be visible on their phone or speaking with someone else. Ensure that if you are in proximity with others either in the workplace or home environments that those people are warned of the needed isolation during your session. This is not because of the fear that others may come into shot or that when the microphone is open that others are heard, but primarily so all participants attending the session can concentrate and fully participate without unnecessary distractions. Never argue during a session, as not only is it distracting in a way that may set a hostile mood for the rest of the session, but the session may also be recorded and it is not an appropriate event for others to observe during a session.

Always remember that when a participant has an open mic during a session, brevity is essential. The principal of the three B's: Be Brief, Be Bright, Be Gone. Be brief in what is said and needed to be said. Be bright and upbeat with positive overtones and manner. Once you have finished, be gone. Finish what you have needed to say and be silent and/or move on.

Most of the already well-established face-to-face interpersonal protocols remain the same in an online conferencing situation. Courteous respect and no agitation, bullying or verbal abuse should be tolerated by the facilitator or participants. If a participant or participants continue to be disruptive and argumentative and have not responded to reason or warning, then the facilitator should remove them from the online session. This action needs to be followed up on after the session in a one-on-one discussion with that particular participant. With that participant, the facilitator should reiterate why that participant was removed from the session and inquire if the participant would like to declare why this happened. The facilitator may wish to instigate conflict resolution procedures if the participant and facilitator feels it's necessary.

If any participant must leave the session prior to completion, then the facilitator must know prior to the actual session commencement. If a participant does not attend or leaves early with or without notification, then the facilitator needs to make a note on their session or course file notes concerning an attendance ledger.

Virtual Backgrounds

A fundamental basic for a facilitator or participant is the choice of virtual background. In a learning environment, it is important to have a low-key, static virtual background. The reason for this is that users of an online conferencing platform generally have access to a photo or video of their choice to use as their background. If the participants or facilitators use as a virtual background a scene that is too distracting or even offensive for any participant or facilitator, then it should not be used. A virtual background should be pleasant to the observe. However, in no way should it be distracting or thought occupying. The virtual background should also typify the personality, character or profession of the participant. For example, a facilitator may choose to have a scholastic or academic background such as a bookshelf or library and dependant on the course may choose a background more specific like a broadacre farming background for a course or session in horticulture is both relevant and possibly inspiring to the participants. Usually the video grabs used as virtual backgrounds should only be short but if they are too vibrant and distracting, they should not be used, especially by the facilitator. Too much colour or contrast of colours can be distracting.

A basic formular for the use of virtual backgrounds in an educational/academic online environment is simple: use a background that is pleasant to look at but also complements the presenter or participant and is relevant or topical to the session being presented.

The facilitator or participants should not change their background during a session as this also may distract the participants especially if the facilitator is sharing their screen, which could hold information that may include video grabs or a PowerPoint.

The facilitator is the presenter and as such the participants must be focused on what is being presented and not be distracted by extraneous visuals that may misdirect a participant's concentration.

Chapter 25

On Your First Day

Ice Breaker

A comment, phrase, joke, pun or action designed to relax and put at ease both class participants and the trainer as an opening remark to a first day class.

You know your participants are in the classroom. But you haven't earnt ownership of your classroom yet. The door is open and as you near, you are stunned by the lack of noise. Chatter and even the shuffle of chairs and paper is missing. You pause briefly as you stand in the doorway and scan the room. You enter the room, focussed on the front desk where you left your paperwork, including class notes, resources and your personal reference material that you put there over an hour earlier.

That will be the quickest you will ever enter a teaching environment, not because of the growth of apathy or familiarity but because nerves and adrenalin of this first day will decrease as you skip into a smooth but suitable normality of purpose, direction and routine.

You stand behind your desk, eyes down, fiddling with papers that serve no purpose other than buying time and settling the first day butterflies. Slowly looking up, you scan the back of the room, being careful not to make eye contact with any of the equally nervous participants. For days you have been rehearsing your opening words that now seem buried in the terror of the first day. Hesitantly, barely audible, you utter to the back wall, 'Good morning and welcome to Better Workplace Communications.'

As you begin to explain the structure and content in brief for the entire six-week course, still to the back wall, one participant interjects with, 'So, who are you?'

What Not to Say

With a nervous smile you reply, 'Well, to all the good-looking people in this class, I am your teacher Josh Edwards. To those people with limited good-looks, I'm still your teacher however, a little less committed.'

You eagerly await the expected jovial response to your attempt at humour. There was none as your gaze flittered from face to face. Not even a smile or reciprocal eye contact. Nothing.

Josh gave himself a major setback with his opening. In Josh's opening nervous comments, he had immediately set a profile of himself in the minds of the equally apprehensive class. What he thought was humour and, in another situation, may have been received as such, felt like painfully irrelevant and potentially idiotic banter. This is followed by mutual embarrassment and alienation. This paradigm may last a few hours, the length of the course or a trainers entire teaching career.

Josh thinks back to the advice he was given regarding the use of an ice breaker to open a new session with a new class. 'Tell them a joke or an anecdote that will prick their interest. Get them onside with a funny comment. Get them laughing and you have them for life.' Well, it failed in a big way.

The ice breaker is an important tool to be used carefully and thoughtfully. Remember that a new tradesman and a new tool often have difficulties, as does an experienced tradesman with an old worn-out or out-of-date tool. The best line of action is if you're unsure of the makeup of your class or even the topic your teaching, then refrain from using an complicated ice breaker that has not been well thought-out.

All Participants are Created Equal

A class of participants is made up of many intricate variables, including age, gender, previous education, geographic location, heritage, nationality, religious beliefs, cultural beliefs, relative cognition and many more. In a class of fifteen participants, there may be so many variables that it is virtually impossible to attempt an ice breaker without the risk of offence towards someone.

A trainer cannot and should never assume that a poorly thought-out ice breaker will not offend someone. A lot of trainers narrow-mindedly assume that all participants share their own ideals and world views and that they would readily accept the humour or comments given by the person of authority standing at the front of the class. Humour to some may be an offence to others. Don't assume aligning personal views when considering comment or humour.

What Can you Say?

Before you attempt an ice breaker there are some vitally important pieces of information that you must know.

Introductions – Do not be afraid to take time to familiarise yourself with participants, whether in a workshop, seminar or class environment.

Know your topic – Be proficient in knowledge, skill and understanding of the topic to be presented. This will give you confidence that will be observed by your participants and grant you authority through respect over time.

Know your participants – Hopefully you will be briefed prior to training on what the general make up of participants is. You should be aware of who the clients are and the various paradigms that they represent. For example, workplace staff undertaking professional development, management staff, participants from employment agencies, incarcerated inmates or a mix of many varying backgrounds and reasons for being there.

Know the training provider organisation – It is important that you have a full understanding of the training provider that you are delivering the training for. Is it government based? Is it affiliated with a religious group? Are they a private enterprise organisation? Are they a not for profit incorporated organisation?

This knowledge may determine not only the type of icebreaker or general banter you can or should use but also help you to determine what is and isn't appropriate speech throughout the entire training/education process.

Icebreakers can take various forms and seldom need to be attempted humour or risqué comments. An opening remark related to general course or facility housekeeping will suffice. For example, explain where the toilets are located and where the exit doors are, and where any emergency assembly areas may be located. This is still deemed an innocuous icebreaker and is the start of a general conversation. Begin the two-way flow of communication by asking if anyone has any questions they would like to ask. While this initial banter is taking place, it gives you opportunity to observe and listen to the participants and begin to formulate initial profiles of the individual participants. This is only the initial conversation and just like you, the participants will also be nervous. Do not formulate and determine an individual's profile on the initial and brief contact. It may not be accurate and may vary greatly from the individuals normal baseline behaviour.

Don't Try to be Funny

We have all been in training of some sort were the facilitator/educator commands the participants with wit and humour. It could be jokes, puns or anecdotal stories. We are impressed with the presenter's quickness to draw everyone to them and we hang off every word that comes out of their mouth. This is not for everyone and if we try to emulate this type of witty, charismatic presenter, we will embarrassingly fall short.

Potentially, the most embarrassing and non-humorous presenter is the one that tries to be funny, yet they do not possess the innate tools to do so such as wit, timing, appropriate personality and discernment.

False bravado can come across as an overcompensation for first session jitters. Bad advice from misguided friends, associates or mentors can steer a trainer down a path they may never recover from. They may never obtain or regain the respect and authority that is needed as an education facilitator.

When a facilitator/trainer becomes more comfortable with participants, then it is possible that they can introduce positive and affirming personality traits in the form of humour or anecdotal stories into the learning environment. This sets a precedent for participants to enter into similar banter. This must be well-controlled, as uncontrolled banter can be distracting, disruptive and damaging to the designated scope of learning.

If you choose to use humour as an icebreaker or throughout general delivery, ensure that you choose a non-offensive joke, pun or anecdote that will not offend any groups, ideologies or marginalised people. Ensure this by consulting a peer for review and affirmation.

A simple rule to go by for icebreakers is know your topic and know your participants. When in doubt, don't do it. Always double check yourself with what you plan on saying. Again, the basic formula for a facilitator/presenter is:

Know your topic->Know your Audience-> Know your Venue (TAV)

On the first day, refrain from humour as an ice breaker. Choose general topics as a simple, non-offensive way to engage participants in a brief discussion. Good topics are the weather, sport, non-contentious news topics of the day (avoid giving opinions), or a general experiential story that give no personal information.

Chapter 26

Fatal Attraction: The Dangers of Attraction, Fraternisation and Infatuation

As humans, we possess our unique individual personality and character. Each one of us project our many differing traits into the world. This happens in all facets of our lives: family, social, professional, sporting and even in the training/learning environment. This is a normal human interaction process, common throughout the world. An individual observes traits presented by another individual's personality and character that they like and are drawn to them, just as others may not like what they observe in someone else and place barriers against that individual.

In a training/learning environment, you have like-minded people confined in a relatively controlled environment brought together for a common purpose through similar goals. This can be a comfortable, happy, pleasant situation as well as a frustrating, stressful experience. After a while, both participants and presenters relax and allow more of their personality to present itself towards others. These may and may not appeal to others and this too is a natural facet of human interaction and reaction. However, issues may arise were two individuals are drawn to each other and take that mutual appreciation and attraction to a different and potentially nonprofessional level.

This mutual attraction may have already existed prior to both participants enrolling into a course of training or education program. If this happened between participants within the learning environment, then there is very little you as a trainer or as a representative from the governing training organisation can do about it, nor should you. The only adverse issue arises when their behaviour, both verbal and nonverbal, impinges directly on themselves or other individuals within that learning environment. If the words or actions between the two mutually attracted individuals has a negative impact on the learning experience of others or themselves in the learning environment, then the facilitator should speak privately with both individuals in an informal meeting. The facilitator should ask that they both be discrete with their relationship in the training/learning environment. This awareness may help them to self-manage and moderate any amorous behaviour that may be perceived as distracting and disruptive to other participants in the group.

Authority and Confidence can be Attractants

If the attraction is from a participant towards a facilitator, the situation must be dealt with as soon as that issue is identified and confirmed as the intent of the participant. Inside the training/education environment, such behaviour must be discouraged by the facilitator immediately. This scenario ideally should be dealt with in the presence of a third party, preferably by a staff member or another trainer of the same gender as the participant in question. An informal discussion should be undertaken with the participant and the third party. However, the trainer should not dominate the discussion. The scope and concern around the issue should be explained by the third party, ensuring clear dialogue, respect and lack of embarrassment is maintained as much as possible. This may be a very delicate situation to address and the individual's dignity must be maintained as much as possible. There must be a suitable outcome strategized that allows the participant a clear option to continue in their education in a comfortable environment, whether that is in the current training environment or other tenable arrangements. This may mean transferring to a different class with a different trainer, or a completely different training provider.

A facilitator is placed into a position of governing and informative authority, showing intelligence and empathy. This itself is attractive to some individuals and may be a catalyst for an individual being drawn to the facilitator. This is apart from other personality and character traits as well as physical appearance presented by the trainer. Often the trainer will encourage and praise an individual participant as they feel it is a necessary part of the participant's education development. This may be perceived by the participant as personal and intimate affirmation. The trainer can observe this misguided interpretation by the participant and how that may evolve into infatuation on participant's part. They see you, the facilitator, as a source of comfort and positive affirmation. This may be something they have been lacking in their personal life and they see you as filling the gaps in their lives in a positive way.

In another scenario, it may be the trainer/facilitator that is drawn to a participant within their education/training group. If this attraction manifests into verbal and nonverbal interaction and is or isn't reciprocated, then an extremely inappropriate and unprofessional situation exists. This behaviour should be stopped immediately before professional and personal integrity is compromised, damaged or irreversibly lost. Under no circumstances is it acceptable for facilitator to show signs of flirtation, affection or other amorous behaviour in the learning/workplace environment. This may cause serious implications for both the trainer and the participant as well as the training provider organisation. A trainer may be faced with serious conflict of interest matters and may be faced with discipline, demotion or even dismissal.

Most government or private adult education organisations have their own code of conduct policies and procedures dealing with trainer/educator misconduct and inappropriate, unprofessional behaviour. The scope of this code of conduct may vary between organisations. However, they fundamentally align. Within these documented policies and procedures will also be the discipline and dismissal protocols relating to inappropriate behaviour in the learning environment. This too may vary between organisations but essentially align. Code of conduct variations may occur between education bodies due to the core nature of the organisation. For example, religious or other private education providers may have code of conduct variations that align with their vision and mission statements as well as their own constitution. There may also be variations due to differences in governmental legislation or cultural differences. It should be noted that in the majority of situations, government legislation dictates code of conduct policies and procedures, whether the organisation is a government or a private education provider.

The Facilitator's Behaviour

The facilitator should maintain a degree of polite aloofness with relation to facilitator/participant interactions. Physical, personal and intellectual boundaries should be maintained.

Physical

In most adult education environments, there should be no reason for a facilitator to physically touch a participant unless enacting a hands-on demonstration. For example, as part of a health care training session such as first aid or beautician training.

Perhaps through nerves or familiarity, a trainer may find that they consciously or unconsciously touch a participant. This of course may be a circumstantial action; however, the receiver of the physical contact may either not wish for the contact to take place or may be uncomfortable about it. The facilitator's best course of action is to follow the advice of 'When in doubt, don't.'

Personal Information

As stated previously, a trainer/facilitator is in a position of leadership and authority. This does not mean that the facilitator is any less vulnerable to manipulation, coercion or interrogation from unscrupulous or inquisitive participants. These participants may ask the facilitator to disclose personal information. Their motivations can be varied, including admiration, jealousy or attaining a feeling of power over or equality with the facilitator.

It is imperative that the facilitator does not disclose personal information or organisational information relating to operation or security. This can be considered a breach of professional and personal confidence.

Avoid disclosure as it can put the trainer into a vulnerable position with participants whose motives may be less than honourable.

Intellectual

As a facilitator, you have been placed in that position because of acquired knowledge, skills, experience and knowledge transferral skills. It is easy for a facilitator in a position of authority to feel overly empowered and at times overly self-assured or even arrogant. It is important as a facilitator to self-evaluate and constantly monitor your own self-awareness and emotional intelligence (EI), ascertaining a professional balance of motive and agenda. Recall the reason you are a facilitator and the professional guidelines that holds.

Chapter 27

Compliance through Policy, Procedure and Legislation

The Governing Training Authority

Governing or registered training organisations (RTO) are providers and assessors of nationally recognised and accredited training courses that have been registered and recognised by an overseeing government authority. Only authorised and registered training providers can issue nationally recognised qualifications. There are thousands of government endorsed training organisations around the world. To be an authorised training provider in any country, an organisation must abide by strict government enforced rules, responsibilities and regulations. This ensures that the quality of vocational education is consistent and of a high and recurrent standard.

Training organisations register with their respective government bodies so that they can present nationally recognised training that may lead to accredited and non-accredited qualifications for participants.

A registered training provider must request the scope of registration detailing:

- The area/discipline that the training provider wishes to focus (if not a broad scope).
- The specific training or assessment it intends to deliver.

- The fields or industries in which it may deliver training or assessment.
- The maximum level of qualifications it may issue to ensure that a registered training provider continues to deliver quality training and assessment.

Accredited and non-accredited education / training is overseen by a governing or department registered authority and must abide by the legislative requirements of that governing body on a continual basis. This accountability is achieved through regular audits and reporting.

Organisational Compliance

Organisational compliance is the process of ensuring that an organisation and its employees follow the laws, policies, regulations, standards and ethical practices that apply to your organisation. Effective corporate compliance will cover both internal policies and rules as well as federal and state laws. Through contract and disclosure, staff and contractors must abide by internal and external compliance regulations/legislations.

Therefore, there are two areas of compliance for most organisations and in particular those dealing with vocational education.

- External – Legislative compliance
- Internal – Staff, contractors or other affiliates

It is usually a very onerous and detailed procedure for a vocational training organisation to be awarded registration as an authorised provider of education and training. Then the guidelines set by the governing body for that registered training organisation to maintain registration is just as stringent and, in some cases, more arduous than the original registration process. Maintaining a quality of delivery must be adhered to by that training provider as an organisation. Every approved accredited course must be justified for re-registering, other potential governing body requirements may include:

- Number of registered courses on the organisation's scope of delivery.

- Level of qualification of each subject on the scope for that organisation.
- Identify number and demographics of completed and prospective participants.
- Identify management and administrative staff and qualifications.
- Identify the number of trainers overall and per specific area of study.
- Show any and all staff development that trainers have undertaken on a consistent and relevance basis since the last accreditation assessment.
- Audit training facilities/environments for suitability and health and safety regulations administered by the relevant government authority.
- Ensure that courses being delivered still meet relevant industry currency and requirements.
- That the training provider through its trainers and assessors is adequately assessing participants and collecting as much assessment material as possible to ensure participant has attained a level of knowledge, skill and understanding to be deemed proficient in that particular course of study.
- Trainer compliance.

If you are employed by a registered training provider in any capacity, including management, administration, trainer/assessor, contractor or ancillary staff, you must abide by all internal organisational compliance requirements and all external organisational compliance legislations, policies and procedures.

Trainer compliance requirements may include:

- Adequate and consistent assessment undertaking.
- Timely submission of required documentation.
- Accurate and presentable personal and class record keeping and reporting.

- Ensuring all health and safety policies and procedures are adhered to for self and participants.
- Update of personal skills matrix and regular industry and academic currency.

There are three major steps to follow regarding personal/industry development:

1. Participate in training. Attend workshops, seminars or enrol in a relevant course of study. Read industry journals and papers. Observe someone who excels at a skill needed.
2. Practice. Continually review the industry and academic currency you have obtained.
3. Get Feedback and self-assessment. Objectively ask for and receive feedback. If appropriate, implement any suggestions that may better your understanding and practical application of new skills. Through self-assessment, objectively determine any practical areas of improvement that you could make. Be cautious with too vigorous self-assessment, as a lot of individuals tend to be overly critical of themselves. Always have an area of self-assessment checked by a peer or someone who knows you well for confirmation before implementation.

Participant Compliance

Upon enrolment, a participant should sign a document declaring that the participant agrees to abide by that organisations policies, procedures and regulations. In doing this they also must abide by external legislations that the organisation is governed by. Some of the external and internal compliance legislations, policy, procedures and regulations that a course participant must abide by may include:

- Health and safety regulations
- Cultural and discrimination awareness
- Violence, harassment and bullying in a workplace
- Safe and respectful use of provided equipment

- Attend punctually within the scheduled delivery times
- No drugs or alcohol on premises
- Submit all assessment on time
- Wear appropriate and suitable attire

It is imperative to the viability and ongoing registration that all three organisational 'stakeholders' remain compliant.

Accredited Training

Accredited training is training that leads to a formal qualification such as a certificate, Diploma, Advanced Diploma or in some cases, graduate certificates.

Accredited training can only be delivered by registered training organisations that own the course or who have permission from the course owner to deliver it. Accreditation of a course of study is an official recognition of the status of an educational qualification by a government endorsed training provider. This gives the qualification legal status, as a bona fide qualification for employment and education purposes. In many professions, accreditation is critically important as a career asset, and for education as a qualification for further study.

Non-Accredited Training

Non-accredited training may not lead to a formal qualification and may not result in a certificate, diploma or advanced diploma. However, it may result in a letter of completion or attendance or that person has acquired the intended skills, knowledge and understanding that are the outcome of the training.

Non-accredited training may be part of an organisation's staff development or to acquire new skills/knowledge learned or an existing skills/knowledge update process.

In some cases, the knowledge, skills gained or even participation in certain non-accredited courses may be part or contribute to similar accredited courses. Therefore, an individual may gain some recognition or credits towards an accredited qualification. This will depend on what the qualification is and what the scope of studies are for the registered training organisation.

Training Packages

The difference between training packages and accredited courses is training packages are a group or family of courses created and approved under government framework and compliance often referred to as training package qualification. Nationally accredited courses are created privately by an individual or group.

In short, a training package is a group of courses that is developed by a service skills organisation. This organisation or group of individuals are employed by a government or government agency to create qualifications around particular industries and provide a framework that qualifies people on a national level working in those industries.

Nationally accredited training courses are courses that have been designed privately by an individual, group or business that has been commissioned by a government agency. If an individual, group or business wishes to have their course made nationally accredited they must present it to appropriate government department for assessment and approval. Once the course is approved, it then becomes nationally recognised and any student/participant who completes all the course requirements including assessment tasks, is then qualified to work in that industry.

Once a course becomes nationally accredited, it remains the intellectual and commercial property of the creator and can be sold to registered training organisations for delivery to their own students however, this puts the purchaser in the position of adhering too course compliance and all other regulatory conditions to be able to deliver the course.

Assessment Tasks and Gathering Evidence

To attain completion of a course of study and receive accredited qualification or non-accredited status, a participant must successfully attend the nominated sessions and duration of course delivery and complete all requires assessment tasks such as observation, demonstration, Verbal, written or through mixed mode assessment and evaluation.

There may be many delivery and assessment variations between training organisations and between courses of study and the respective industry requirements. There is also variation in delivery and assessment methods attached to individual course requirements that fulfil both external and internal compliance needs. These are academic or industry based.

If the course of study is practically and therefore industry-based, then delivery and assessments are through observation and demonstration. If the assessor deems the participant's demonstration has fulfilled the competency standard required, then the participant should be deemed competent in that area of learning. The trainer must assess competence through observation and match against written requirements. Once the demonstration task is completed by an individual then the assessor must tabulate observation results into a formal report to be submitted to the training organisation for formal verification of the individual's completion and competence in that element of learning.

If the assessment task requires a participant to present information to the assessor verbally, then the presentation environment must be suitable for that participant to be heard and understood by the assessor allowing for accurate assessment and recording of competencies the assessment environment should be free from extraneous noise and distractions that may interfere with the verbal assessment process.

Both the assessor and the individual being assessed need to be comfortable and feel that they are in the best environment for a fair and accurate determination of competency by the learner. If one or the other are not comfortable about the assessment location, then assessment needs to be rescheduled to an environment mutually acceptable for the learner and assessor.

Usually in a training and assessing environment, an individual's competency is determined by progressive written assessments throughout the duration of the course/learning experience. These assessments may be in the form of regular written tests that are specific to elements being studied or through work manuals aligned with scheduled areas of study.

Mixed mode assessments are used to holistically assess an area of study that may require variations in assessment methodology. This usually accommodates for theoretical components as well as practical assessment requirements through demonstration and assessor observation and evaluation.

Assessment variations may be required if the participant has a physical, psychological or cognitive impediment of some kind. Any impairment to learning by a participant should have been declared at enrolment or discerned by the training organisation and the assessor. Once the impairment has been identified/disclosed then an assessment strategy can be implemented with the participant's consent. Areas of delivery and assessment variations may include:

- Access and egress to the learning environment
- Seating position within the learning environment
- Lighting
- Sound
- Appropriate delivery and assessment mediums
- The use of appropriate trainer/assessor
- Translator
- Carer or support person
- Access to appropriate specialist external support
- Organisational Support

Chapter 28

Keeping records

Organisation

To maintain organisational and industry compliance, a registered training organisation must collect and maintain accurate records of delivery and assessment as well as any variations or incidents that require reporting. An organisation must also keep up to date records of current qualifications of trainers and assessors as well as any staff development undertaken by them either internally or externally as part of their personal skills matrix updating and currency.

For compliance requirements an organisation must keep accurate records of not only their trainer and assessors but also participants and courses delivered to maintain industry relevance and currency.

Trainer/Assessor

The trainer must keep current records of their individual qualifications. They must maintain and continually update their personal skills matrix by including any staff development such as industry or academic courses, workshops or seminars as well as notification of journal subscriptions and articles that may benefit the trainer with their delivery and assessment.

File Notes

A trainer/presenter should also keep record of any issues that arise while delivering a session including inappropriate behaviour by a participant or any breaches of the training provider's policies and procedures including health and safety and physical location issues. These trainer file notes are an important resource for any educator for self-improvement, governance and accountability.

It is unnecessary to write many pages regarding a particular issue or point of record, but a note should be written even in point form as a reminder and brief record of noteworthy issues or potential improvement to personal and resource delivery for that educators sessions. The file note must have and identification heading such as:

- Name
- Date
- Time
- Location / Venue
- Course
- Session
- Stakeholders involved (if required)
- Summary (even point form) of 'noteworthy' information
- Reporting protocols (if required)
- Action required
- Follow up

Not only is a file note a very good best practice resource for personal and educational development, but a file may be asked for in a court of law depending on the matter and how it relates to that particular issue.

Participant

A trainer/assessor should advise all participants to maintain personal records of their attendance as well as tasks and assessments undertaken.

They should include any issues they may have experienced while undertaking written submissions. It is also advised that participants keep both hard and electronic copies of any submitted assessments as well as any competency records presented by the assessor. A participant may also like to make record of their own perceptions and interpretations of the course, session and trainer as an aid to the course delivery sessions including content and presentation. These notes should be brief notes and should not take up the participant's time during a session. These notes may be vitally important when topics are reviewed for an assignment or exam.

IV Postface

Conclusions are Just the Beginnings

Adult education can be very rewarding and a source of tremendous personal growth and considerable self-awareness and self-fulfilment.

The hope is that this book has gone towards equipping you with skills, knowledge and understanding to have greater confidence when you find yourself in front of a participant or a group of participants. It is both an honour and privilege to be able to pass on your knowledge, understanding and practical skills.

In review, there are some key fundamentals to adhere to. Firstly, never prejudge a participant or measure them against your own personal experiences. Remember, you do not know what has gone on in their life up to the time they sit before you in a learning environment. Nothing should be perceived as typical. Always enter into a participant/facilitator relationship with the understanding that you may learn something from their personal professional life experiences. This is knowledge you can apply to industry or your role as a facilitator.

Please do not take this privilege for granted or look at it as a mundane task or obligation to your employer. See it as a pivotal link to a participant's personal and professional wellbeing.

This book is just the start for a new adult educator or reaffirmation for those who have been in the industry as they move along their adult educator journey. Take time to review and make corrections in your own delivery style if you feel it is needed. Don't be afraid of change in who you are as an adult educator, in the new skills and knowledge you wish to share or in how you should and need to present those new knowledge and skills.

What you do counts and can make a difference to that one starfish washed up on your beach.

Acknowledgements

I would like to thank family and friends for their support, encouragement and ability to lovingly advise and correct.

I would like to acknowledge the painstaking work that my editor Michaela Teschendorff Harden has undertaken in helping to pull this book together. Her patience, advice and ability to keep me focused and on the straight and narrow is greatly appreciated and must be acknowledged.

I wish to recognise the work of graphic artist Meg Hanlon for all graphic design in this book.

Glossary of Words, Terms and Phrases

Algorithm (Qualitative & Quantitative): A set of procedures or a list of rules to follow for completing a specific task or solving a problem. Qualitative methods are descriptive whereas quantitative are numerical.

Andragogy: The method and practice of teaching adult learners; adult education (Vocational).

Apex of delivery: The point in a presenter's delivery where the session reaches its most important part. This could be pivotal to the session or even the whole course. It can be emphasised through word structure and through verbal and nonverbal expression.

Apex point (Trainer): The trainer or facilitator should hold the primary focus of participants in an educational environment. Even during audio-visual or guest speaker presentation, the primary trainer should always hold a focus point of authority within the training environment.

Assessor: An assessor is someone registered by a relevant education/training quality assurance organisation (usually a government body) that measures competence against specified national qualification unit standards and qualifications.

Baseline of normal behaviour (BNB): Is the typical or expected behaviour of an individual, group or system in a presented situation. This baseline varies from individual to individual and over time or event, may change temporarily or permanently.

Baseline of normal speech (BNS): The verbal presentation of an individual under normal circumstances. This may be determined by topic, environment and audience. Consistent conversational oscillation familiar to the speaker is considered a BSN.

Behavioural assessment: A practical and functional assessment that is a continual process of collecting information with a goal of identifying the environmental variable that may identify problem or target behaviour.

Behaviourism: A theory of learning which states that all behaviours are learned through interaction with the environment through a process called conditioning. Therefore, behaviour is simply a response to environmental stimuli.

Body language: A range of nonverbal signals that are used to communicate an individual's feelings and intentions. This includes posture and facial expressions. An individual's ability to observe and understand others body language can help to interpret unspoken issues or feelings of others.

Buy ups: A canteen-like service within correctional facilities administered by custodial staff where inmates can purchase some items from their work allowances. This may include chocolates, soups, packet noodles or tins of tuna.

Choral repetition: Where a teacher, facilitator or learner models language so that a group of learners repeat information needed to be retained. This may be in drills, chants or songs.

Constructivism: A theory that says that learners construct knowledge rather than passively absorb it. The learners experience the world and reflect upon those experiences. This builds their own representations and inputs new information into pre-existing knowledge.

Conversational Oscillation: Verbal communication is not regulated by tone, pitch or volume. In general conversation between face to face individuals, there is no set pattern of verbal communication. Individuals speak in peaks and troughs (oscillation), not monotone.

Verbal communication varies and is controlled by the individuals intent and the message they want to transfer and how they want to transfer it.

Delivery Session: Providing education through activities such as lectures, tutorials, seminars, practical demonstrations, laboratory sessions, clinical practicum sessions, fieldwork, supervision, workplace instruction or other teaching methods.

Delivery tool: A resource or instrument designed to help educational participants/students learn, engage and improve their educational experience. Some examples of delivery tools may include Audio-Visual presentation equipment, practical resources aligned to the topic being taught, written papers or books supporting what is being taught.

Discernible intent: To form or create an intent based on a perception determined by observation, interaction and senses such as sight, smell and sound.

Domino effect: When a negative or positive attitude, or even an argument, is taken on by the other participants until they agree negatively or positively with the instigator or group of instigators. One by one they accept what was presented before them as fact. This may or may not be factual.

Dropped the ball: A consistently performing individual within the learning environment that for some reason has suddenly changed both attitude and education outcomes to a lower standard from their BNB.

Dispute system design (DSD): The creation and establishment of a series of dispute resolution processes to aid organisations to better manage conflicts. This may be in a structured form such as organisational policy and procedure as part of an ongoing best practice protocol.

Emotional intelligence (EI): The ability to be aware of, control, and express one's emotions, and to manage interpersonal relationships judiciously, empathetically and with courtesy (Goleman, 2005).

External training: Training undertaken for an organisation by a separate organisation or individual that specialises in the specific training required. This may be done by a Registered Training Organisation (RTO) or by a qualified consultant that is not an employee of the organisation.

Facilitator: An individual who helps bring about an outcome such as learning, productivity or communication. This is achieved by providing an individual or group of individuals indirect or unobtrusive assistance, guidance or supervision.

File notes: Information kept by an individual to record proceedings, issues or events that are noteworthy, and can be used for information recall. In an education environment, notes are kept on file as a record of issues, incidents or as best practice to gain information on improving sessions delivered.

Fold Change Detection: A measure that describes how much a quantity changes between an original and a subsequent measurement.

Fringe dweller: An individual that is present at a training/education session, but does not often contribute during sessions. These individuals may or may not have full understanding of what is being presented and should not be considered not competent until further research undertaken.

Haptic: Tactile learning from a sense of touch (hands on).

Have a Chat/Motormouth: This is an individual who is very talkative and presents as gregarious. They feel that this distracts others and the facilitator from identifying potential or perceived weakness in the participant. On the other hand, they may be just talkative and really enjoying the session and feel they would like to contribute and/or have lots of questions.

Host Organisation: An organisation that provides structured and supervised practical experience for students for the purpose of improving their vocational readiness.

Innate Behaviour: Behaviour that is not necessarily knowledge or skills gained but is present from birth. Some call it instinct.

Internal training: Training undertaken by an organisation for staff or associated organisations specifically linked to a particular industry/vocation. The training is done internally by qualified experienced existing employees.

Knowledge recall: The process of remembering information. It is an efficient way of moving information from short term to long term memory so that you can easily draw on it again when you need it most, such as an assessment, assignment or a presentation.

Learning/education outcomes: The gaining of knowledge, skills or technique through experience, demonstration or presentation/learning.

Lecturing: To present a structured/formal talk to individuals or a group of individuals.

Liberationist: A theory where the student is at the centre or focal point of the classroom instead of the teacher. Pupils have more say in what they learn and how they learn it.

Macro environment: Learning facility, registered training organisation, other external organisations where training is held, like a factory or farm.

Micro expressions: Facial expressions that may occur in a fraction of a second. This involuntary or unaware emotional leakage exposes an individual's true emotions.

Micro environment: Immediate training area, such as a room, chair, table, whiteboard.

Mirroring Effect: A behaviour were an individual subconsciously imitates the gesture, speech patten, tone, volume and even mood of another individual in their presence. This often occurs in both social and professional situations, particularly in the presence of close friends or work colleagues. It has also been a conscious and deliberate tool used in conflict resolution.

Mob Mentality: The ability of humans to adopt behaviours and follow trends based on their circles of influence. This can appear in many forms, whether through blindly following someone in class or gaining support against a fellow student, facilitator, or study material.

Modelling and Demonstration: Whole-of-class teaching strategies that rely on interactive practices such as the use of resources and asking relevant but probing questions. Participants working in pairs or the use of whiteboards and post-it notes may be part of a Modelling and Demonstration strategy of learning.

On the spectrum: The spectrum consists of a group of disorders of development with life-long effects and that have in common a triad of impairments in social interaction, communication, imagination and behaviour. Communication can be challenging as can be the use and interpretation of body language.

Paradigm: A set of ideas that display an individual's standards or perspectives. The word is common educational, scientific and business worlds.

Paralanguage: The presence of vocal effects such as tone, pitch, volume, pace, inflection. These may accompany or modify the phonemes of an utterance and may communicate meaning and intent.

Participants: Individuals being present, active and engaged in an educational environment.

Pecking order: An informally established level of ranking is among a group of people. There are many factors that contribute to the established hierarchical order such as intellectual, physical attributes and authority through displayed aggression (actual or passive). This may occur in any group of individuals from corrective services inmates to a class on corporate senior managers.

Pedagogy: The act of teaching. Theories of pedagogy increasingly identify the student as an agent, and the teacher as a facilitator. Conventional western pedagogies, however, view the teacher as knowledge holder and student as the recipient of knowledge.

Personal Frame of Delivery (PFD): The imaginary frame that contains the presenter's normal stance and use of hands and arms during delivery.

Pragmatism: Considers words and thought as tools and instruments for prediction, problem solving, and action, and rejects the idea that the function of thought is to describe, represent, or mirror reality. Pragmatists contend that most philosophical topics—such as the nature of knowledge, language, concepts, meaning, belief, and science—are all best viewed in terms of their practical uses and successes.

Proactive: An instructor trying to eliminate a problem behaviour before it becomes a bigger and potentially spreading problem.

Profiling: The analysis and recording of an individual's behavioural and psychological characteristics with the objective of assessing or predicting an individuals intent or capabilities. This can be determined by written, verbal or nonverbal observation.

Qualitative Non-Numerical Algorithms: Involves the collection, use and analysis of non-numerical data, meaning information such as text, video or audio. Analysis is conducted to interpret concepts, opinions or practical experiences. It can be used to gather complicated insights into a problem or generate new ideas and perspectives.

Rote Learning: The memorising of skills and techniques based on repetition. The basis of this specific method relies on repeated recall of repeated observation and practical application.

RTO (Registered Training Organisation): An organisation that delivers recognised accredited and non-accredited training in the Vocational Education & Training (VET) sector.

Schemas: Compartmentalizes information received into categories for storing in long term memory. This makes storing information / knowledge easier and therefore easier to recall.

Semantics: A branch of linguistics that focuses on the study of meaning. Semantics study ways in which the meanings of words can be related to each other (synonyms, homophony, etc.), ways in which the meanings of sentences can be related to each other, and ambiguity.

Social Constructivism: A theory of knowledge according to which human development is socially situated and knowledge is constructed through interaction with others.

Spotlighting: When a facilitator/trainer singles out an individual participant, sometimes continually and exclusively. That individual is seen to be singled out or 'spotlighted' by the facilitator/trainer. This can be embarrassing and humiliating to the participant as well as other observing participants.

Syntax: A sub-discipline of linguistics that studies the structure of a sentence. It studies the set of rules, principles, and processes that rule the structure of sentences in any language. Here the term structure of sentence refers to the word order.

TAV: Know your **T**opic, Know your **A**udience, Know your **V**enue. These are the foundation pillars for educators.

Their 'go to': A behavioural trait in an individual that may be expressed verbally or non-verbally. A coping mechanism when an individual is in doubt or trying to avoid stress. For example, to divert from a line of questioning related to a session topic, the participant may become unduly argumentative in an aim to derail the poignant conversation away from a topic they are uncomfortable with. Another example would be a participant who consistently claims illness to avoid sitting for an exam. Sickness then becomes there habitual 'go to' strategy. Note: A 'go too' is only valid if it becomes habitual to that individual over a series of times and under certain circumstances.

Trainer: Generally, professionals that possess skills and knowledge to help people gain or progress in jobs, tasks or specific responsibilities.

Training area: An identified or dedicated area for the specific purpose of training/education. This may be attached to a Registered Training Organisation or a commercial organisation that has a specific and industry related training area.

Under Active: Where the facilitator or learning institution does not hold the participants/students at the core or their interests. The participants discern an obvious apathy from the facilitator/instructor.

Workplace Experience: Short term placement in an organisation to gain some knowledge and practical experience and that organisation and the industry they represent.

Author's Quotes Throughout the Book

'If a man picks an apple, he is fed. Give him an education and he can pick the apple without the worm.' p.iv

'Learn so that you may teach.' p.v

'To hear someone is to listen. To see someone is to understand.' p.28

Know your Topic, know your Audience and Know your Venue (TAV). p.62

'If you are using a lectern or presenting from behind a desk or other object, then you incorporate the height and width of the lectern into your personal frame of delivery (PFD).' p.41

'For some people death is preferable to speaking in public.' p.81

'Emotional intelligence is the key to both your personal and professional success and development.' p.94

'Lying seems to empower them. They gain gratification at being able to create a false reality.' p.118

'This in essence is one of the hardest situations to deal with an individual as it focuses on the belief by a participant that they have formulated in their own mind a 'false reality' that is ingrained in their own psyche and a real and very present and seemingly supported reality.' p.132

'When an individual is continually asked for input or general comment, that individual may feel isolated or 'picked on'. This is called 'spotlighting'.' p.136

'What we hear from others is important however what we see in others is vital.' p.29

Definition: Verbal Communication is a type of oral communication wherein the message is transmitted through spoken words. Here the sender gives words to their feelings, thoughts, ideas and opinions and expresses them in the form of speeches, discussions, presentations, and conversations. p.30

'Your voice expresses your personality, and your tone portrays your mood.' p. 32

'How you say something can be more important than what you are actually saying.' p.34

Definition: Nonverbal Communication can be defined as communication without words including behaviours such as facial expressions, eyes movement, touching, and tone and volume of voice as part of 'paralanguages. Less obvious messages such as dress, posture and spatial distance between two or more people can deliver important nonverbal messages. p.39

'It is important what is being said however, it is vital what is not being said.' p.39

Be Brief Be Bright Be Gone p.157

Nonverbal punctuations (Including exclamation): While full stops, commas, exclamation marks and many other symbols adorn and organise our written languages. In face-to-face presentation the use of appropriate verbal and nonverbal behaviour can just as easily apply the correct and necessary grammar to those participants listening. p.45

'Verbally Punctuate your speech to create better meaning to the structure and form of your delivery.' p.141

Definition: Intelligence can be defined as the ability to obtain knowledge in an adaptive situation, while cognition means general awareness and the ability to gain knowledge in particular ... For example, someone with an exceedingly high IQ may have severe cognitive impairment. p.146

Baseline of Normal Behaviour (BNB). Over time it is always best for an observer to use the BNB to ascertain consistent variables and therefore a need for concern and potential intervention to help the participant any way that the facilitator can. p.154

'A comment, phrase, joke, pun or action designed to relax and put at ease both class participants and the trainer as an opening remark to a 'first day' class.' p.171

Authority and confidence can be attractants. p.177

Meekness is not weakness, it is power in control. p.111

Safety and possibly anonymity in numbers (Mob). p.110

References

Cambridge University Cambridge Dictionary (2024). *A haptic device creates a physical feeling such as a push or vibration so that you know, for example, when you have pressed or touched something on a screen.* Cambridge University Press (Internet & Telecoms). (p.158)

Cicero, M.T. (2022) *Eye contact and movement. 'Ut imago est animi voltus sic indices oculi'.* The face is a picture of the mind as the eyes are its interpreter. Cicero (106-43 B.C.). Arpinium. Notre Dame Philosophical Reviews (Schofield, M.). Oxford University Press. (p.43)

Comenius, J.A. (1592-1670). *The concept of audio-visual education.* Encyclopedia Britanica Nov 10, 2023. (p.155)

Dickens, C 1859, *A Tale of Two Cities*, 7th edn, Penguin Classics, London, England. (p.1)

Eiseley, Loren, 1969, 'The Star Thrower', *The Unexpected Universe*, Mariner Books, Boston, Massachusetts. (p.iv)

Eysenck, H 2012, 'Personality and individual differences', *Science Direct*, Vol. 103, pp. 74-81. (p.90)

Freire, P, 1970, *Pedagogy of the oppressed*, New York: Continuum 1970. (p.26)

Goleman, D 1995, *Emotional Intelligence*, 1st edn, Bantum Books, New York City, New York. (p.94)

Goleman, D 2005, 'EQ or IQ', *International Comparative Jurisprudence*, vol. 2, no. 1, pp. 55-60. (p.94)

REFERENCES

Knowles, M 1984. The Adult Learner: A Neglected Species (3rd Ed.). Houston, TX: Gulf Publishing. (p.27)

Mayne, D. W 2022 *Nonverbal Communication.* Rotary Leadership Award (RYLA) Participants Manual. (p.29)

Mayne, D.W 2022. *Verbal Communication.* Rotary Youth Leadership Award, 2022. Participants Manual. (p.39)

Mayo Clinic 2022, 'PTSD Symptoms and Causes', *Mayo Clinic,* viewed 13 December, <https://www.mayoclinic.org/diseases-conditions/post-traumatic-stress-disorder/symptoms-causes/syc-20355967> (p.116)

National Institute of Adult Education (England and Wales), 1970. *Adult education.* A 1970 report, from the National Institute of Adult Education (England and Wales). (p.19)

noun: emotional intelligence (EI) Piaget, J. (1936) *Constructivism is based on the pedagogical research* of Piaget (1890-1896). (p.25)

The Encyclopedia Britannica 2023, *Vocational education is instruction intended to equip persons for industrial or commercial occupations, necessary skills on the job.* Encyclopedia Britannica (History & Society) Booker T. Washington. Last update Nov 10, 2023, (p.18)

The Oxford English Dictionary 2023, *Andragogy is the method and practice of teaching adult learners; adult education.* Oxford University Press. (p.18)

Thorndike 1911, Pavlov 1927 and Skinner 1957 *The theory of Behaviourism* came from *pedagogical research.* Xavier University – Anteno de Cagayan. Course Code: Ed.4.2023 (p.24)

Vygotsky, L. 2005, 'The development of social constructivism believing that learning was a collaborative process between participant and facilitator', *International Education Journal,* vol. 6, no. 3, pp. 386-399. (p.26)

Workplace Health and Safety (WHS) NSW 2020, *Work Health & Safety Act Amendment (Review).* ACT 2020, Schedule 2. (p.51)

www.ingramcontent.com/pod-product-compliance
Lightning Source LLC
Chambersburg PA
CBHW041138110526
44590CB00027B/4062